WALKING IN
DOMINION

Monica Ramey

MY PRAYER FOR YOU

My prayer for you:

I pray that something you read in this book will cause you to rise up and overcome whatever obstacle is holding you back from being the person God designed you to be. I pray that you would be forever changed, and that shackles of the past, self-imposed limits, or limits put on you by others would be broken off from your life.

I pray that you would say yes to whatever the process looks like for you to become who you really are, and that you are inspired, equipped, and move boldly to purpose and destiny.

I pray that you would run hard after the dreams that God placed within you, and that you begin to rule and reign, and walk in this thing called Dominion in every area of your life.

In Jesus's name, amen!

Prologue

All this Dominion stuff started for me as I was driving on the interstate, weeping as if someone was dying. That someone was me. My thoughts were all over the place, and it felt like I was bleeding out emotionally. I was smack dab in the middle of an emotional crisis, and it wasn't pretty. I was coming to the realization that I was going to be divorced for the third time. How would I recover from this, and why couldn't I just get it right? It seemed like I kept going in circles and getting the same type of guy, just packaged in a different body.

This time I thought it was going to be different. I now had God on my side and was sure He was going to intervene and save my marriage. I mean I gave my life to Him, He has good plans for me, right? (Jeremiah 29:11 NIV) Why did it seem like everything was getting worse instead of better, and where are all these good plans?

Husband number three seemed to have started loathing me when I became a Christian, and there was nothing I could do to fix it. He didn't want any part of my new life, and our relationship seemed like it had an unseen force pushing us apart like two magnets opposing each other. (Ephesians 6:12 NIV)

All I knew was if someone had to go, it wasn't going to be God. This time, I was not letting go of Him. I had seen too much. My eyes were open to the reality that not only was God real but there were dark spiritual forces, and they were working hard at stopping me in every area of my life.

I continued driving down the interstate, crying out for answers and trying to figure out what was wrong with me. I was pondering all the times I had been betrayed by infidelity. I had been through the wringer already with abuse. Every relationship had a similar tone—physical, verbal, or emotional abuse.

Those same patterns reared their ugly head in every male relationship I was in. There must be something wrong with me. I'm not good enough—I need to be better. Thoughts of self-loathing and guilt were bombarding me, and I was being carried away to a dark place in my mind. My emotions were all over the place, as I was trying to figure it all out, when out of nowhere a voice from somewhere deep within me started speaking.

I heard these words: *Let us make man in our image and let them have dominion. (Genesis 1:26 KJV) Monica, you have never*

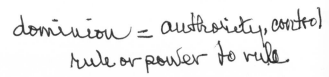

had dominion. Everyone has had dominion over you, and I am going to teach you dominion.

And just like that, a peace came all over me and every tear dried up. I couldn't cry anymore. I remained quiet the entire ride home as I was trying to wrap my head around what had just happened. It was God! I was wonderstruck; the God who created the entire universe not only just spoke to me, but He knew me by name.

Now, you would think that I went home and researched this Dominion thing, but I was too caught up in the fact that He spoke to me and knew my name. I had just been validated by God. He knew me and cared about me. That was all that mattered to me at that moment.

That was also another clue into the brokenness of my life. My need to be valued, affirmed, and loved trumped everything else. I didn't know it at the time, but this was a major theme running through my broken life. I was getting ready to begin a journey of self-discovery and inner healing. I would learn about my wounded soul and how it impacted every area of my life—how I thought about myself, how I related to others, and even how I related to God. I was about to walk into something new—this thing called Dominion.

CHAPTER 1
My Father

MY DAD WAS 54 AND MY MOM ONLY 18 WHEN THEY were married. They eloped in fear that my grandparents would try to stop it. He wooed her and swept her off her feet by making promises of money, security, and world travel. He was suave and a fast talker. He was exceptionally good-looking, and he was on a mission to win her over. She was captivated by him. He made promises to her that he never kept. Quite honestly, he was looking for a trophy wife. Their marriage didn't last. They had my older brother, and after I was born, everything fell apart.

She left him, and we moved in with my grandparents. They did the whole battle-it-out-in-court thing for a while, with it resulting in my mom being awarded custody of us. My mom was a sore subject to bring up around my dad. He never got over her and had major unresolved issues about the whole thing. He was very bitter. Mom eventually married again, and through that union, we got an awesome addition to our family, a little brother!

My dad always wanted a girl. I remember him telling me that several times. He even had a nickname that he liked to call me (I hated it). He called me Sissy. We would have visits with him on holidays and some weekends, until I was around 10 years old.

He treated my older brother differently than me. Maybe in my dad's mind and his old-fashioned ways, he was treating him "like a boy." He may have thought showing affection to his son wasn't manly. I really don't know for sure. We were little kids, so I can only speculate.

Nevertheless, as siblings, we had a sort of a love/hate relationship. It felt a lot more like hate on my end. Some of my earliest memories are of him hitting me. He would hit me, and I would cry. My mom or whatever adult that was around would reprimand him. Instead of being satisfied that he got in trouble, I somehow felt responsible for his punishment. I felt guilty and terrible when he got in trouble. I wanted to rescue him even though he had just hurt me.

That scenario became a pattern for the way I handled relationships with men. I gravitated toward broken, abusive men and became a verbal, mental, or physical whipping post for them to punish and work out their unresolved issues. Somehow, in my subconscious, that old, <u>false responsibility issue</u> would arise, and I found myself overlooking and allowing the destructive behavior.

I'm not a psychiatrist, but I believe my brother felt or saw that our dad treated me differently, and that caused jealousy in him. From the stories I've heard, the anger toward me started very early on, and I was kept in a baby bed a lot for safety.

That behavior continued until we were out of high school.

Eventually, our dad stopped picking us up for his visitation schedule. I remember the day we waited for him at the end of our super-long driveway. We waited and waited, but he didn't show. Finally, I walked back up the driveway to tell mom. My brother stayed at the bottom of the driveway for a long time that evening, trying to assure himself that dad would show up, refusing to believe that he wasn't coming. He never did. We wouldn't see him again until we were in our teens.

When my brother turned 16 and got his driver's license, the first thing we did was plan a secret road trip to go find our dad. We were both excited and nervous. I secretly hoped that it would be like one of those reunions you see on TV—one where the parent sees the child whom they haven't seen in years, and they run and embrace each other with open arms.

This trip was a big deal because we had to travel across the state line. We found the house, got out, and knocked on the door. After what seemed like forever, he came to the door and stood there looking at us and then said, "Yes?" He didn't even recognize us. To his defense, it had been a long time since he had seen us, and we looked totally different, but the little girl in me wanted her dad to show her how much he missed her and loved her.

We didn't even get invited in. My brother told him who we were, and then his countenance changed and he smiled. He was glad to see us, and we would take any scrap we could get. He talked a lot. I don't remember anything that he had to say. I think it was just nervous chitchat.

It sort of felt like we were talking with a stranger. I wanted him to like me, and to act like it. I wanted him to make a bigger deal of me than he did. There was no hug, reconciliation, or the fairy-tale scenario that I drummed up in my head. I expected him to be overcome with emotion and welcome us with love and affection. There was none of that.

He did ask us to come back, and come back we did. He took us out to eat the next time. I became disappointed on hearing him tell the story of how he helped the waitress out because her son needed an operation. Dad was helping out our waitress financially. I was jealous—he didn't help us like that. Why did he care about that lady's son and not us? I wonder if he was telling her all the things he told my mom.

As I look back, I think that my dad loved us, but it was a selfish love—the kind that had to work out best for him, or he was jumping ship. Through my healing journey, I also recognized that he just didn't have the capacity to love me the way I thought I needed to be loved. I wished things could have been different, but I accept things for the way they were. I don't hold any resentment toward him anymore.

There was a lot going on in my wounded soul. I remember another time in my teen years when I had an argument with my mom. She told me if I hated living with her so much, I should go live with my dad. So I called her bluff and started packing my bag. She gladly drove me to his house.

We pulled up and knocked on the door; when he opened it and saw my mom, he started combing his hair. He looked at me, then back at her, and asked, "What's going on?"

Mom told him that I had decided I wanted to live with him. Without any hesitation, he said, "I don't have enough room for her." Then he directed the conversation back to my mom, asking her if she was remarried. He seemed more concerned about the way he looked than he did about anything going on with me. That day was devastating to me emotionally.

CHAPTER 2
The Setting of the Sun

I GREW UP IN CHURCH. FROM A VERY YOUNG AGE, I always knew God was real. I could feel His presence, especially in church. My mom had us there every time the doors were open. We went Sunday morning, Sunday night, and Wednesday night. My mom's twin sister co-pastored a church with my uncle. It was a small lively little church, and I loved going there.

I always knew God was supposed to be a part of my life. I could sense His presence and felt spiritual things since I was very small. I remember picking up my Bible before I could read, opening it up, and knowing that whatever it said on the inside was special. That book was special. (2 Timothy 3:16 NIV) I talked to God, prayed to Him at night, and knew He could hear me. I just knew it.

When I was about seven years old, we moved into a mobile home park. I would ride my bike through the streets and sidewalks, feeling the wind blow on my face. I would take my hands off the handlebars and feel so fearless, like I didn't have a care in the world. I loved it there.

The theme song of the movie *Annie* was my favorite. I watched that movie and fell in love with the character. I would sing the theme song over and over again. I can remember being at the playground, swinging so high that I thought I would flip over the bar of the swing set. I would yell out at the top of my lungs, "The sun'll come out tomorrow; bet your bottom dollar that tomorrooooow…there'll be sun…." Heck, I WAS Annie! I had so much confidence and was free like a bird. All my days consisted of playing with my friends, imagining and creating stories to act out. I could pretend to be anyone I wanted to, and that's exactly what I did!

Sometimes, I was the girl from the movie *Grease*. I had a best friend, and we got out our "pinkest" jackets and became the Pink Ladies. We rode our bikes all over the neighborhood. We were so cool. We owned those streets. We went around everywhere, singing the songs from *Grease* and would take turns being the lead character. Every day was an adventure!

We played outside until the streetlights came on. That was the time we all hated—the dreaded streetlights. I can recall days of being at the playground and lying on the ground for what seemed to be hours, just wasting the day away, watching the puffy white clouds form into awesome pictures right before my very eyes. I loved doing that.

During that time, I was also on a gymnastics team. I felt like I could fly. Gymnastics was everything to me. The floor was my favorite. I could do handsprings and tucks and dreamed of being just like Mary Lou Retton.

Dorothy Hamill—the famed ice skater—was another hero. I begged my mom for months to take me ice-skating. She said I was too little and that it would be too hard. I drove her crazy asking her to take me ice-skating—I just KNEW I could do it. I could feel it in my bones. In my mind, I saw myself gliding effortlessly all over the rink.

Finally, she conceded, and I found myself putting on those clunky brown skates at the local ice-skating rink. She helped me lace them and then laced hers and my brother's. We all held on to each other and anything else we could find, and wobbled onto the ice. I slowly put my skates on the ice rink floor, got a quick feel for it, and just like I had pictured in my mind, was gliding around that ice rink, while my mom and brother were glued to the side of the rink and falling all over the place.

I felt like Dorothy Hamill. I knew I could do it! I was gliding all around the rink! My mom still tells that story of how surprised she was when she saw me skating with ease. But I saw myself skating long before I put the skates on. I just did what I saw myself doing.

• As I look back, SEEING myself doing things was an inner marking of who I was and what I was designed to do. I saw and knew things about people and situations. As a child, those visions and insights were natural to me and just a part of who I was.

As I grew up and encountered trauma and pain in my life, those things I saw for myself weren't trustworthy anymore. I started believing things that others spoke over me until I didn't trust or believe what I saw or who I was anymore. I wish I could tell you that my childhood was filled with more movie characters, songs, and adventures, but other than a few vacations with my grandparents, that's about all I can recall of the good old days.

One thing was for sure—no matter how loud I sang, my sun stopped coming up one day and Daddy Warbucks didn't show up to rescue me. On the contrary, someone else showed up.

We were still living in the mobile home park when my mom met him. He was an evangelist preacher from out of town, who had been invited to speak at our church. My aunt introduced him to my mom, and the two of them became fast friends. They started dating soon after that. Everybody seemed to like him, and I remember him winning all our hearts over fast. It seemed like he was the missing piece to our family. We were so excited to have him come into our lives. He took us on adventures, played with us, and got involved in our lives. He eventually asked my mom to marry him, and she did. His name was Larry.

Soon after they were married, we bought some land connecting us to my mom's twin sister's property and purchased a big modular home that looked like a log cabin. It was amazing—at least we thought so.

Everything was new and exciting for us. It was like we were going to have a new life with a real dad—one who would stick around and even get to live with us. Larry was adventurous and fun. He wrestled with us, played outside, and took us everywhere. My mom seemed like she was happy too, maybe for the first time ever as far as I had known. We were like a real family, and we couldn't have been happier.

We had three-wheelers and motorcycles. He made sure to give us things to make life fun for us kids. He even talked my mom into buying a trampoline for me for my birthday, which was another one of my lifelong dreams at eight years old. It was an indoor trampoline that we kept outside, but I didn't care. That thing was the all-time greatest gift I had ever received. I lived on it and loved it with everything in me. I spent countless hours on it. I remember my mom having to make me come inside. I mean, I LOVED that trampoline.

I also loved my new stepdad. We went to him first for everything because he was the one who would say yes! He built a treehouse for us behind our house with a swing and a handle on it that was attached to the tree above the platform. We would take turns swinging off that platform for hours. We had our very own piece of heaven up on that hill. My mom finally seemed to have the right person in her life, and we had a real dad.

We all felt safe and loved. Larry took care of us like we were his own kids. We all looked up to him. He was a long-distance truck driver. When he was home from road trips, he always made sure to pour out attention and affection on everyone. He would make my mom a special cup of coffee in the evening before we settled in for the night.

I can recall several occasions when he woke me up in the middle of the night. He would tell me that my mom had asked him to give me medicine, because I had been coughing. He was stepping up to take care of us. When he was in town, he drove us to all our sports events and practices. We were just like a real family.

It felt safe having him in the house since nighttime was a big struggle for me. I was terrified of the dark. I could physically feel fear and what I knew of at the time to be just scary dark things. Shadows darted in my room and moved on the walls of my bedroom, and I saw them at other places I visited. At night, I saw things in my dreams that could have only originated in the pit of hell. They were of a demonic nature, and the demons were usually attacking or tormenting me. This stuff was sheer and utter torment, and I dreaded closing my eyes at night. I had so much fear and anxiety. It seemed like I slept with one eye open.

Nightmares had been a part of my life for as far back as I could remember, and several were recurring. One of the terrors that showed up the most in my sleep was the demonized girl from the movie *The Exorcist*. She chased me and tormented me from about the age of five until my early twenties. Some adult in my family had the bright idea that it would be OK to watch that movie with small kids around. I remember watching it, hearing the girl speak with that crazy voice and holding my ears, closing my eyes, and humming "Jesus Loves Me" to drown out the voice. I was paralyzed with fear. Years of my life were stolen just from viewing and hearing a few minutes of a movie.

Much later in life, I discovered the reason that things of that nature had such a profound effect on me. Even as a young child, I had an "awareness" of spiritual things. It is a gift called "discerning of spirits" that I would discover, along with other gifts, much later. (1 Corinthians 12:10 KJV)

There was one specific nightmare that I repeatedly had while living up on that hill. I don't remember having it until my mom and Larry got married.

In the dream, someone was trying to pull my arm over the blade of a guillotine to cut it off. Right before the blade would slam down on my arm, I would somehow manage to get free and pull my arm out of the trap. I can't count how many times I had that nightmare.

CHAPTER 3

Big Bad Wolf

SLOWLY, THINGS BEGAN TO CHANGE, AND LIFE ON the hill became a dark scary place. It would be the beginning of a different little girl and a different life. One day, we heard that the police had been at a neighbor's house, and we found out that someone was peeping into their windows. We were all on high alert after that. We started hearing reports of someone peeping into other windows in the area surrounding where we lived. That was a frightening time for us with my stepdad out of town for days at a time while my mom was home alone with three kids. She started making sure she knew our whereabouts and would make us come inside before dark.

I was also going through puberty, and it seemed especially hard for me. My life and my body was changing. I started acting out in strange ways, trying to hide the new changes in my body. I was completely and totally ashamed of it, and I didn't want anyone to look at me. I started wearing layers of clothing, even in warm temperatures.

I had no idea why; I just did. I knew something wasn't right about it, but I had to do it. I wanted to be covered up all the time and especially didn't want any of my newly forming body parts to be viewed.

I was always racked with fear and started a habit of bizarre nightly routines. I felt comfort and protection and a sense of control when I went through my bedtime routine. Every night, I pulled a fluffy blanket out of my bedroom closet, rolled it up, and stuffed it under my door. I tried to wedge it in as far as I could. The lock on my door was broken, and I guess I thought somewhere in the back of my mind, I was keeping the boogeyman out. I put on my extra layers of clothing and got ready for the final phase of the ritual. I would get in my waterbed, pull the covers up, and tuck the blanket into the crevices as far as it would go until there was only room at the top for me to climb in. Then I would scoot down until I was tucked all the way in.

I don't know how long I did this, but I remember stuffing the covers under the door one night, and something made me stop and question what I was doing. I thought, *What in the world am I doing? What's wrong with me?* I had the thought that I was going crazy. I knew there was something not normal about me. I knew it everywhere I went at every minute of the day. It never left me.

The beginning of the end of our life on the hill began to unravel. It happened during a summer break from school when we went on a vacation to Gatlinburg, Tennessee. My brothers and I were super excited while we loaded the car. It was about a five-hour drive. We were going to leave in the evening and drive straight through the night. Little did I know that the trip we were taking would change the world as I knew it, and I would never be the same.

The vacation would include a decent hotel with an indoor pool and lots of amenities, visiting a theme park, and anything else that caught our attention. After getting the car loaded and everyone packed inside our little vehicle, we started our journey. My mom drove with my stepdad on the passenger side. After a few hours, my stepdad decided to give up his front seat to sleep in the back. We had the back seats folded down so we could sleep through the night. I said that I wanted the front seat, but my older brother had seniority and won the spot.

That simple changing of seats set in motion the loss of an innocence, never to be regained. My stepdad went to sleep, my little brother beside him and eventually me on the other side. I laid there bright-eyed with excitement for our upcoming adventure. There was no way I could sleep. My mind was already in Tennessee!

After some time, my stepdad's arm shifted very quickly. He went from having his arm thrown over me to sliding it under my shirt, holding my stomach. I wasn't asleep. I had been lying very still, so I would not wake him because of the proximity of our sleeping quarters. I don't know how much time passed before I was startled again. This time his hand moved up my shirt, and his thumb rubbed back and forth over my chest.

Panic and confusion hit me, and I shot up from that position and sat behind my mom in the driver's seat. I asked her if I could sit in the front. My brother heard me and argued to keep his position, and won. I sat up behind my mother as close as I could get to her seat, completely crippled with fear all the way to Tennessee. I couldn't articulate what had just happened to me; all I knew was that something wasn't right. Why did he do that to me? I was afraid and didn't want to be near my stepdad. I could feel him looking at me. I knew he wasn't sleeping. He was watching me.

We made it to the hotel, got settled in, and went to sleep to get ready for our first day of vacation. My mom and stepdad had their own room with a door connecting to ours. My brothers shared a bed in our room, and I had a big bed all to myself…lucky me. I was a sitting duck and didn't even know it.

That next day we went exploring around Gatlinburg. We decided to knock out the theme park. We got there, and to our surprise, it was a dud. It was still in the beginning phases of opening back then and didn't have a lot to offer. It seemed more like a place for grownups instead of kids. We were all disappointed.

We did find a small roller coaster ride and got in line. Panic set in. Who would I ride with? My stepdad volunteered to ride with me. My insides were screaming "NOOOOOOOOOO," but I was powerless. I couldn't find my voice to say no or even words to explain why I didn't want to ride with him. I will never forget being whipped around by this ride and using every muscle in my body to grip the bar of the cart so I wouldn't touch my stepdad. That ride was torturous.

We also did indoor skydiving and got our pictures taken while flying in midair. I was always a daredevil, and under normal circumstances, this would have been an absolute delight for me. It was far from a delight. Everything we did on that trip was torment. I didn't want to be looked at or have attention brought to me. Something had changed. I was afraid and aware of something on a whole new level.

I looked back at that skydiving picture years later and felt grief because I remembered exactly how I felt while I was in midair. Instead of the exhilaration of flying, I was flooded with shame and fear because I knew the yellow sky diving suit was clinging to my body and my stepdad could see me. I felt so exposed and so ashamed. I couldn't look him in the eyes anymore, and I didn't.

That night back at the hotel, I woke up startled by a noise. I could feel fear in the dark. I looked over my shoulder—my stepfather was sitting with his back turned to me, facing the wall, and he was completely naked. I instinctively started coughing to signal to him that I was waking up. It worked! He scurried off.

The entire night was that exact scenario happening over and over. One time I sat up and grabbed the stale leftover soda sitting on my nightstand and then shoved some candy fudge into my mouth to let him know that I was wide awake. What was he doing? Why wouldn't he leave me alone? I didn't understand. I knew something wasn't right, and I wanted him to leave me alone. I was so afraid.

On the last day, we ventured out again, but I was just going through the motions. I was worn out from not getting enough sleep and emotionally numb. I didn't know, but I was stressed from carrying the weight of what was happening to me. I was trying to control situations such that I could have very little contact with my stepdad. I became obsessed with finding ways to avoid him.

Our final night in the hotel was when everything fell apart. I woke up to him sneaking in our room, but this time was different.

He wasn't leaving when I coughed. He wasn't leaving! I had to step up my game, so I got louder.

The next time he came in the room, I sat up with my eyes closed and started coughing as hard as I could and as loud as I could. It worked, and he left again.

The sun was starting to come up at this point, and I wasn't laying back down for more torment. I sat on the side of my bed, looking at my brothers who were sleeping so peacefully. At that moment, something happened that has been forever etched in my mind. Something no child should ever have to encounter.

The only way I can describe this is tell you exactly what I saw. It would be the first of many times that I saw something that most people don't ever see in their lifetimes. I sensed the presence of evil like a wet blanket covering me, and knew I was being watched. I dropped to my knees, feeling almost paralyzed by fear, and managed to crawl over to the bed where my brothers were sleeping.

Fear had taken over, and for the life of me, I don't know why I looked, but I did. I glanced over my shoulder, and what I saw was my stepdad, but it wasn't my stepdad.

He was standing on top of the toilet bowl completely naked and touching himself as he watched me. Over his entire form was a huge, dark, evil creature that was encasing him. It was evil and unlike anything I had ever seen. It was in him but towering over him as well. It wasn't my imagination. It was real; it happened. I saw it with my eyes, and I will never forget it. I didn't look again. I was physically shaking, and my muscles were weak. (Job 4:15-16 NIV)

My heart was beating out of my chest, and the next thing I knew, I was whispering to my older brother with both of my hands around his forearms, clinging for dear life. "Wake up!" I was squeezing his arm, pleading with him in a whisper for him to wake up. He told me to leave him alone. I was NOT letting go until he responded with a yes. I squeezed even harder. I said these words as I squeezed, "Please wake up; let's go to the pool. PLEASE WAKE UP, please, please, please, please, please!" I think he finally picked up on the urgency in my voice and sensed something was wrong. To my surprise, he jumped up, grabbed his things, and I followed him out of the room.

He kept asking me what was wrong. I couldn't tell him until I knew we were in a safe place. I didn't know where he was taking me, and I didn't care. I just wanted away from that situation. We ended up in the sauna room past the pool area. I dropped my head in shame and said, "Larry keeps touching me."

To be honest, I don't remember what else we said, or if we said anything at all. I just knew I was safe at that moment. I cried what seemed like rivers and let out all the fear, pain, and stress of the past few days. The two of us sat in the steamy sauna room, hiding until we could think of what to do next.

While I was sitting in the stuffy miserably hot sauna, sobbing my heart out, out of nowhere, the door opened wide and there stood Larry staring wide-eyed as he immediately asked, "What's wrong, Monica?"

It was the shock of my life. It felt like an electric shock of fear gripped all the nerve endings in my body. Terrified and covered in shame, I dropped my head. There wasn't anything I could possibly do to function at that moment. Fear owned me.

The next thing that happened was nothing short of amazing. I don't know how my brother came up with this on the fly, but he stood up and shouted out loud, "SHE STUBBED HER TOE!!!"

Then he picked up his foot and planted it in the door, and firmly pushed the door all the way shut on Larry.

This brother, the one that I fought with my entire existence, was now my hero! He looked over at me and said, "We have to tell Mom." I couldn't take the thought of being exposed even more. I was so afraid that somehow this was my fault. "Nooooooo," I cried, "PLEASE don't tell her. We can't tell ANYONE!" I made him swear that he wouldn't tell her. I was terrified of what was next. Fear of the unknown was too much to bear.

Finally, he stood up, and I followed him back up to the room. On the way, we passed Larry who had already gone back to the room and woke my little brother. The two of them were playing bumper pool.

I don't know how long we were in the sauna before that door flew open. After watching me wake up my older brother, Larry must have rushed to get dressed, get my little brother dressed, and then rushed downstairs to find us. I don't know, to tell you the truth, because I was in the middle of a crisis. Larry knew this was all getting ready to come crashing down. He had to have known that I was telling my brother everything. To go back to the room, we had to pass Larry and my little brother. I kept my head down in shame.

We made it back inside the room and my mom walked over to us. She saw the looks on our faces and my puffy eyes, and asked what was wrong. Silence. Well, silence for about 30 seconds because my brother, who swore to secrecy, broke his promise and said, "We have to tell her."

"Tell me what?" she asked.

"Larry has been touching her." He just blurted it out.

I couldn't look at her. Shame was all over me like I did something wrong. Was she going to hate me? I felt guilty, ashamed, and numb.

Everything after that is a bit of a blur. I remember we packed up immediately, got in the car, and drove home. We drove in complete silence. I rode home with a pillow on my lap with my face buried in it. I didn't look up. I never wanted to look up again. Ever. I felt so dirty and somehow responsible for what had happened to me—like it was my fault.

Larry was with us as we drove home. Why was he still with us? Why didn't we leave him there?

I didn't understand any of this, and I didn't know what to do with myself. I just knew what he did was wrong. I had no idea why he was doing what he was doing. I had no frame of reference and didn't understand why he would not leave me alone. I was being exposed to something that I was not equipped to handle.

Larry drove us all the way home. I rode the whole way back with my face buried in that pillow. I couldn't look up, or look at anyone for that matter. I wasn't sure if I could ever look at anyone ever again. I was so ashamed. My mind had already started forming beliefs about the situation. We finally made it back. I immediately went and hid in my room.

I remember hearing Mom's and Larry's muffled voices through the closed bedroom door at some point. I can't recall everything that happened during the next few hours, but I do remember she made Larry leave.

He did not go easily. He tried to convince her that everything would be OK. He would get counseling, and in the meantime, he wouldn't stay in the house. When he wasn't on the road with his job, he would sleep in a camper on our property.

Mom told me recently that he begged her to go to counseling soon after we returned from Tennessee. She thought they could somehow salvage their marriage; Larry was also in fear of going to jail, so he was desperate to stay in some type of good grace with her.

After some evaluations, the psychiatrist diagnosed him as a pedophile. It was the first time my mom ever heard that word.

My family's way of dealing with the situation was to not deal with it at all. They basically pretended it didn't happen, and we all just carried on like nothing was wrong. My mom, grandmother, and grandpa never spoke a word to me about it. If the name Larry was brought up while in my presence, a tension came in the room, and people reminded the one who slipped up by giving him/her looks, as to shut the conversation down. They must have all agreed not to talk about any of it in front of me, but they were definitely talking, and

making decisions about what they were going to do next.

CHAPTER 4

Betrayal

MY GRANDFATHER ASKED IF I WANTED TO GO FOR A ride. This was highly unusual. I don't remember him just inviting me to go for a ride with him. We got in the car, and when we were a little way up the road, he said he wanted to talk to me about something. He brought up the incident in Tennessee. I could tell he was trying to be sensitive with the conversation.

He tried to explain away Larry's touching me. He made excuses for him such as, "Maybe he really didn't know what he was doing when it happened. Maybe he was asleep, and he thought you were your mom—he may have been confused. It could have been an accident."

Total shock—like I had just been hit upside the head! I felt defensive, "It was not an accident." I started to cry. Even my grandpa was not on my side. He was trying to smooth this whole thing over for some reason. It was like he was trying to help me "overlook" all of it and dismiss it. I knew it was not an accident.

I was ashamed of even talking about things of that nature with my grandpa. I still had no way of processing what happened to me. I just kept saying, "It was not an accident. It was not an accident."

When we got back, I went into my grandparents' bathroom to hide. I locked the door and just cried. This was an angry cry. I felt hatred, shock, and confusion. I remember thinking that they must not believe me. I was so angry. Nobody was on my side. It would be years before I could identify the source of the anger—it was betrayal. This wound went deep into my soul.

These things did happen to me. Why don't they believe me? My grandfather was supposed to be on my side. And he wasn't. Every grownup I looked to for protection was betraying me. I must not be valuable. Don't you protect the things you value?

Something in me died that day in my grandparents' bathroom. I realized I was alone. I remember feeling very rebellious. I decided to stop caring about anything or anyone. No one believed me. Something switched in me that day.

During that same time, my mom and grandmother took me for a ride. They drove to an area that was well known for being one of the worst low-income housing project developments in our area.

This was one of the places you would hear about on the nightly news for crime. There were kids running wild, jumping on cars, screaming, cussing, and fighting with each other. It was dirty and run down. I didn't know what we were doing there.

My mom said, "Monica, this is where we are going to live if you don't let Larry come back." My grandmother was just quiet. She didn't say a word, but I could tell by the expression on her face that she was in full agreement. What? Was she serious?

I hung my head quietly and cried, "Nooooooo..." I only remember feeling anxiety and fear that I would be the one responsible for our family having to live in such a terrible place.

Betrayal on top of betrayal, these events were reinforcing a belief system that something was wrong with me and that I wasn't valuable.

As I look back, the wounds from those incidents at the hands of my family were probably worse than the molestation. My family was all I had; they were my support and were supposed to protect me. (Psalm 27:10)

CHAPTER 5

Rotten Fruit

IN THE MIDDLE OF THIS CRISIS, I WAS SENT TO SPEND the night at my aunt's house. I was looking forward to spending time with my cousin. After dinner, my aunt told us that the kitchen was closed. Later that evening we wanted a snack, so we waited until the coast was clear. We crept into the kitchen, my cousin pulled an orange from the refrigerator, and we scurried back to her bedroom. We hid between the side of the bed and the wall, so we didn't get caught with our goods. As she peeled the orange, I decided to tell her about what Larry had been doing to me and the events that had been unfolding.

To my surprise, she said it happened to her too. It was a heavy moment. It was a shock to learn that I wasn't the only one! While we were deep into the events, my aunt opened the bedroom door. Busted! We were caught! We were caught not only with the illegal orange but also in the middle of our confidential conversation. The surprised looks on our faces must have given us away because when she looked at us, she asked "What was going on?"

I told her everything.

When my aunt found out that Larry was molesting not only me but also her daughter, she went to work questioning the other two kids in the house. Her youngest daughter had been molested too. My aunt called the police.

Everything hidden was coming to the surface. (Luke 8:17 NIV)

One Sunday morning at church, a visitor stood up in the middle of the service and interrupted the speaker. She said that she needed to inform the church that there had been "sin in the pulpit." She said that Larry was having an affair with a certain deacon's wife. She called them both out by name in front of the entire church.

Mom was sitting in the front row when it happened. She was humiliated. Later she said that all she could do was muster the strength to walk out. The shame of that encounter must have been more than she could bear. It was the straw that broke the camel's back. It would be the last time she went to church. Her world just kept crumbling.

One thing led to another, and we eventually found out that Larry was the infamous peeping tom of the neighborhood too.

I started having dark flashbacks at that time, and the pieces were coming together. I began to remember.

I remembered seeing my stepdad standing naked in my bedroom. I remembered hearing footsteps in the hall, my bedroom door opening, and flashlights shining on and off in my face. I remembered waking up with a strange substance dried up on my face and in my hair. I remembered all the "accidental" moments of him standing naked in his bedroom as I passed by the door, and the times he was wearing only a white T-shirt and socks, standing in the dark and staring at me. None of it was an accident.

I eventually realized the reason I could never sleep—the reason I was so afraid of what was coming down the hallway. It WAS the boogeyman I was hiding from when I stuffed the covers under the door and tucked the blankets around me in the water bed. I was subconsciously trying to protect myself. The lock on my bedroom door that was broken "for no apparent reason" was broken for a reason.

I thought about my recurring dream of yanking my arm away before the guillotine chopped it off. I truly believe that that dream was God protecting me from what was happening. My stepdad was taking my hand and touching himself with it, and somehow, I knew to yank my arm away.

Now I know that when he was waking me up to give me cough medicine, it wasn't because I was coughing. He was knocking me out, so I wouldn't know what he was doing to me.

That special cup of coffee he made every night for my mom? He was slipping something into her drink as well. He made a big deal of making it look like he was taking care of her and doing something special for her with her nightly drink.

Eventually, Larry was arrested. The investigators and lawyers wanted all of us kids to come in, so they could hear our testimony. In preparation, my mom and aunt had a private meeting with me in a bedroom. My aunt asked me all sorts of questions pertaining to how Larry had violated me. I was so humiliated and ashamed. More humiliation—now I had to talk about the sexual abuse. Previously, I wasn't allowed to acknowledge any of it, but now I was being asked to disclose everything out loud.

I just wanted all of it to stop. I wanted it to go away, but it wasn't. Now we were going to go to court, and it was all my fault. I knew I was in the way, an inconvenience. My very existence seemed to be a problem. All I did was cause problems for everyone. One lying belief after another was being established like a mighty fortress in my mind.

When we met with the investigators, they quickly realized that asking me to testify against Larry would be even more damaging to me. They ended up using the verbal testimony of my youngest cousin. Larry was convicted and sent to prison. He was sentenced to three to five years but was released early because he was a "model prisoner." We heard later that he was preaching to other inmates while incarcerated.

For many years, we were a family in crisis, and we would move from crisis to crisis as time went on. We didn't tend to the gaping wounds. We just moved on. And you know what they say—hurting people just end up hurting people. And that's just what we did—we hurt each other. Our family was torn in two.

Larry was gone now, but things did not get better. By this time, we had moved and were living about 10 miles away in a small sub-division. It seemed like the people around me were getting back to whatever was normal for them, but for me, life was just different now. I was angry, felt alone, ashamed, and I was trying hard to keep from going all the way crazy. Not equipped to handle any type of conflict, I started reacting to things violently. I just didn't know how to deal with what had happened to me. This went on for years.

Anger would just rise inside me. I'd fight with my mom. Then I'd break things. Usually, it was something she liked. Once, after she left the house, I took some of her dishes and walked out to the street in front of the house and smashed them in the middle of the road. I had some underlying need to punish her. Another time during a fight, I slammed my fist into a glass coffee table. That one required stitches. Another time, I broke a drinking glass, and when that didn't satisfy my rage, I decided to kick one of the shards of glass with my bare foot. You can guess how that turned out.

Lying became a way of life. I lied about where I was going, who I was going with, and what I would be doing. At about 13, I started hanging out with a girl down the street. One day, she stole a quarter bag of marijuana from her brother, and we decided to smoke it. Five hours had passed before we knew it. We had smoked the entire bag of marijuana.

By the tenth grade, I was taking every chance I could to stick it to my mom. I wanted to do what I wanted to do and had no problems lying, manipulating, or bullying to make sure it happened.

During this time, I started living a double life. I was popular and involved in school. I participated in sports, but behind the scenes, I was partying and hanging out with an older crowd. I had my first real boyfriend. It was the first of several dysfunctional relationships that I would get into.

CHAPTER 6
Husband #1

WHEN I WAS 16, THINGS GOT SO BAD DURING THE summer that I ended up in a behavioral health unit for evaluation. I had been having anxiety and sleeping for extreme amounts of time. Something was wrong. My primary care doctor recommended that I go to the hospital for an evaluation and bloodwork. I had NO IDEA what was happening. I thought I was checking into a hospital to have bloodwork for depression. When I arrived, I realized that this was not the case. I was in a hospital for people with mental health issues.

They were bringing in kids on stretchers. I remember seeing girls with their wrists bandaged up because they had tried to commit suicide. I was trying to explain to the psychiatrists and counselors that this was a big mistake. This wasn't where I was supposed to be. Nobody seemed to be listening or caring about what I was telling them. All I knew was I had to get out of there.

The first phone call I could make was to my grandfather. I felt if I could just get him on the phone, he would get me out of there. I called him crying, telling him how I didn't belong in this place. This place was for "crazy" people. I laid the manipulation on very thick.

The next thing I knew, I was being discharged from the hospital. I was never so happy in all my life. In all reality, I was probably exactly where I should have been. I was severely depressed and had even went through months of thinking about easy ways to end my life. I'm sure that my doctor recognized the depression symptoms and acted.

I had suicidal thoughts on and off for a couple of years. I remember being numb and tired all the time. It felt like I had a dark cloud covering me emotionally. Panic attacks would come out of nowhere.

I even remember taking a hammer once and breaking a plastic shaving razor to get the blade out of it. I took the razor blade, locked myself into my bedroom, and just held it at my wrist. I pressed it hard to my skin but didn't have the nerve to do it. I wanted to die, but I was afraid it would hurt.

The background feelings and thoughts of "what's wrong with me" never left. I was tired of fighting. I felt crazy, saw things that weren't there but knew that I was seeing them, and knew things without knowing how I knew. I heard voices and felt things I didn't want to feel. I just wanted out. I wanted it all to go away—all of it.

After getting out of the behavioral health hospital, I went for a visit to my aunt's house, who was now living in Florida. My mom and I were still struggling in our relationship, and I welcomed the break after what I had just went through. The break was even better than expected when I realized how easy it was to party when I made it to Florida. I had more freedom there than I did at home.

I was invited for a visit to my uncle's house one night. He had been divorced from my aunt for some time then and was living about 10 minutes away. I hadn't seen him in years. When I got there, he offered me a beer and I took it. The rest of the evening was a big party. We all hung out in his basement, and I met some of the guys that worked for him.

One guy, in his mid-twenties, was paying extra attention to me. He seemed nice enough and a little more "normal" than some of the other workers who were there. One of the not-so-normal guys ate a palmetto bug after consuming too many adult beverages that night. A palmetto bug looks like a roach but only much, much bigger. I will never forget that night—not only because of that but because the "normal" guy, who was paying me so much attention, ended up becoming husband number one.

I thought it was extra cool that he was older than me. The best part was that he was only in Florida for work. He was from Ohio and told me he would be coming back. My "vacation" ended, and I went back home.

After he came back to Ohio, we continued to date. He was divorced and had two children from another marriage. He seemed mature and made me feel wanted and loved. He wanted to marry me. He was in a hurry about it too.

I went to work trying to convince my mom to sign the papers because I wasn't legally old enough—shy by one year. She held her ground for as long as she could until I finally broke her down and she signed. We set up a small ceremony at a courthouse in a judge's chambers. I was so nervous, but excited too, that I was going to have a different life. I would finally be free.

When I look back, I thought that I was leaving my problems behind, and this marriage would somehow make everything better. I felt like I had been rescued. He was going to take care of me, and my life was going to be better.

The only problem with the whole thing was that all my past, with my pain and problems, came with me, and his did as well. We both had a busload full of baggage. I knew after a few months that it was a mistake. He had a big problem with alcohol, and it intensified as time went on. He couldn't get a grip on it, and I couldn't take it anymore. Our problems together were just too much for me to handle, and I wanted out.

It was over just about as fast as it started. I came back home with my tail between my legs, embarrassed and ashamed. I failed in marriage. I needed a new direction for my life.

I always dreamed of being a hair stylist. At five years old, I stood in amazement watching a hairstylist at work. I can picture it to this day—the exact moment. It was like time stood still while I watched her. I wanted to do what she was doing. That desire never left me.

I was the girl to whom people came to get their hair done throughout the year for school dances. I had a raw ability inside me to make someone's hair look good, and I loved it!

Since I had already dropped out of high school, and my marriage didn't work out, my grandfather convinced me to go to cosmetology school.

Hair school was easy for me, and I excelled at it. I wanted to learn everything I could about it, and I did. While there, the owner of the college was very hands-on with the students. His name was Mike. He was a phenomenal barber; I loved watching him and gleaning anything I could from him. He recognized that I was hungry and poured time and knowledge into me.

He was unlike anyone I had ever met. He was always positive, respectful, and kind. There was something about him that made me want to listen to everything he said. He had something inside him that I didn't—I couldn't put my finger on it just yet, but I wanted it. I was broken emotionally, and it was a struggle for me to discipline myself to show up every day, even though I loved it. I did just enough to get by; I didn't give it my all until I was nearing the end of my final semester of school.

The owner announced an upcoming competition that would be held in Ohio about 40 minutes from us. It was a real competition. We needed live models, and our work would be judged in two categories—haircutting and an overall makeover with a live model who would walk the runway.

I got with another girl in school who was interested in being my model. I decided on a look for her hair, we purchased an outfit, and I entered both categories. This was a huge deal. The day of the competition came, and I worked on my model in front of a panel of judges. The first category was haircutting. I had never even practiced the haircut. I would cut it for the first time at the competition (nobody knew that but me). I just knew I could cut it because I could see it in my mind.

There was a guy doing a haircut next to me, and I could tell he was going to be a tough competitor. He was and ended up winning the haircutting competition, while I came in second. I was still happy with second place—this was a big competition. I was thrilled!

The thrill of that win had made me push even harder for the next category. It was the biggest event—the overall competition with my live model. I had just given her a fresh new cut, and now we had to dress her, apply makeup, and style her hair. Mike was with me and the rest of our group from school when it was time for the models to walk. He videotaped when it was my model's turn on the runway. The music was playing, and my model emerged.

That moment is one that is hard to forget. It was so exciting! This pale, quiet wallflower, who barely spoke a word in hair school, walked out, and all I can say is that she EXPLODED on that runway like a supermodel!!! She had the walk, the look, the expression— she blew us all away. We were all standing there with our mouths wide open.

After all the models walked the runway, we had a break while the judges tallied up their scores. This was one of the most exciting things I had ever been a part of.

We came back into the building and waited for the awards to be given out. We went through all the awards ceremony for hair, and I received my second-place award for haircutting. I couldn't have been happier. Mike was still videotaping. It seemed like all the awards had been handed out and the event was coming to an end, when I heard them announce the final award for the overall competition. It was the biggest award of the day, and they called out my name and my hair school! My heart started beating a million miles a minute. I WON!!!

The next minute or two seemed to happen in slow motion. We were all jumping up and down and shouting. I looked over at Mike, and he looked back at me with tears in his eyes. He grabbed me and hugged me, and we all celebrated like we had won the lottery.

•That moment became one of the greatest moments in my life. The award was secondary.

The biggest thrill was Mike affirming me. He was proud of me—even moved to tears! I would be forever changed. What he didn't know was that I was so broken, I had never really seen what a healthy relationship with a man looked like. At that moment, he was a dad-in-proxy cheering for me, and it met a need that I had somewhere deep within me. I wanted him to be proud of me. He was one of the first men in my life who didn't look at me like an object. This was different—it was pure.

I started buying and devouring any book I heard him mention. I wanted to be better. I stopped skipping hair school and had a drive to get up on time in the morning. This guy was handing out life skills I needed; I didn't want to miss anything he might be talking about. He had information that made me feel better on the inside, and that was just what I needed.

Looking back, it was so obvious that God placed this man in my path. He was the start of my journey to getting my life back. I had so much more to go through, but those seeds were there. (John 12:24 NIV)

CHAPTER 7
Abduction

MARCH 1ST, 1996. THAT DATE WILL FOREVER BE etched in my brain. It is my younger brother's birthday, usually a day of celebration. This birthday was not enjoyable for him, or any of us for that matter. It was one of the most devastating days of my life.

My son JC was five months old. His dad, Alex and I had been married for a year. The marriage was falling apart. I ignored every single warning sign about this relationship while we dated. Trust me, there were many signs, but I was wallowing in brokenness and was desperate to be loved.

His mother lived in England. She met his father, an American soldier, while he was stationed in England. They fell in love, got married and had a child. She came to the United States with her new American husband. Things didn't work out and she decided she would go back to England with her child, without telling her husband. Alex was pulled back and forth between both countries throughout his childhood. Having parents in both countries also gave him dual citizenship.

I specifically remember having the thought of knowing how broken this man was and thinking that I could help him. A couple of family members tried to talk with me before I married him. One of them said they felt like I should take some more time before I pursued marriage with him. I couldn't be persuaded. I thought that love alone would be enough to heal both our broken pasts.

But wait…there's more! We could have a baby of our own and give each other everything that we didn't get! It would be perfect! I didn't know at that time that people can't give out something that they don't have.

Wow, did I have a lot to learn, and a big lesson was on its way. One of the biggest, most painful of my life. We decided to have a baby, and soon after, I got pregnant.

With good intentions toward each other in the beginning, we quickly found out good intentions wouldn't be enough. Two traumatized souls. "Hurting people hurt people." Things were not good.

We could not go any further without intervention. Things got bad. When we would argue, he would often pick up our son and go into another room with him, like he was keeping him from me. I told him that if we didn't get some type of counseling, I was going to file for divorce. It seemed like that was what he needed to hear. He told me he would and that he wanted to work on saving our marriage.

Alex scheduled weekly counseling sessions for himself. It seemed like whatever he was doing was working because he was even being nice again. Maybe we would be able to make it work after all.

My great grandmother, who we called Nanny, was a woman of strong faith. She had a relationship with the Lord, and we all knew it. She was a prayer warrior, and when anyone got into trouble or anything serious happened to anyone in our family, they went to her so she would pray. (Hebrews 4:16 NKJV)

One day I was visiting her, and she told me she had a dream. In that dream, I fell down on my knees before her, devastated and with an empty baby blanket in my arms, and I kept crying, "MY BABY, MY BABY!!!"

She said she thought it was serious, and she didn't like the dream—it scared her. I heard her loud and clear, but I intentionally pushed it out of my mind. I couldn't even entertain the thoughts of what that dream could mean. So I carried on with my life while seeing warning signs but ignoring them, not wanting to believe that things were as bad as they actually were.

Nanny's health took a turn for the worse. She lived with her daughter and son-in-law, my grandparents. I took care of her for over a year before I was married and also while I was pregnant with JC. She and I were like peas and carrots. I loved that woman, and she loved me.

I had a cute name for her that always made her laugh. I called her Nana Bean because she was always cooking, and somewhere in the mix would be a pot of some type of beans. When I heard her health was declining, I planned to spend as much time with her as I could.

I went to visit her on March 1 and left my five-month-old son with his father. Something was off that day. I can't describe it exactly, but I knew something wasn't right. I left for the 10-minute drive to her house, and when I did, a song came on my car radio, and the strangest thing happened.

I could hear one line of the song coming out of the radio louder than any other parts of the song, like something was wrong with my car radio. It grabbed my attention. The words were: "A ONE-WAY TICKET on a west bound train." But only the words "one-way ticket" were much louder than the other words in the line to the song. It was like they were jumping out of the radio at me. It was very strange. I ignored it. I had an overall uneasy feeling that wouldn't go away that day.

I went and visited Nanny for a couple of hours and tried to help with whatever she needed. I drove back to my apartment, opened my front door, and everything just seemed off. I wasn't sure what I was seeing because it hadn't clicked yet. Things were thrown around and messier than when I had left. The apartment was small, so I quickly realized nobody was home. Had the apartment been broken into? What in the world had happened in here?

Thoughts were racing in my head with what I feared the most, but that was too devastating and traumatic for me to give space in my mind. So I pushed it out. I started to panic. Things were missing. I went to the closet in the bedroom, opened the door, and found that the suitcases were missing. I didn't allow that thought to stay either. I was in denial until I went to the cabinet in the kitchen where all the baby food was kept. Gone. It was all gone.

I came undone.

Someone came and got me and took me to my grandparents. Nanny was sitting in a chair at the end of the dining room table. I ran over to her and fell to my knees, crying, "MY BABY, MY BABY!!!" Her dream came to pass. I wept at her feet.

I knew that I had to stay really close to her because she knew the One who could help me. I wasn't letting her out of my sight. She cried with me for a while and then said, "Come in here." She stood up, and I followed her to the formal living room. It was a sitting room with nice furniture that they didn't really use.

She sat down, and I said, "Nanny, I am going to kill him," along with a few other words that I will leave to your imagination.

She gently touched my arm and said, "No honey, we need to be humble right now. I'm gonna pray." (1 Peter 5:6 NIV) I was instantly quiet. And just like that, she opened her mouth and started praying. Some of it was in English, and some of it was in another language. She was releasing words to Heaven on my behalf. They were sincere and fervent, and coming from a place deep within her. It was the first time I felt like I had a glimpse of hope.

The Bible says, "For he that speaks in an unknown tongue speaks not unto men, but unto God: for no man understands him but the spirit speaks mysteries." (1 Corinthians14:2 KJ 2000 Bible) I didn't know what she was saying half of the time, but I didn't care. I just did what she said and was also trying to figure out the humble thing—to posture myself on the inside and be reverent while she was talking to God.

Everyone else stayed in the dining room and talked amongst themselves about what they thought we should do next. My little brother's birthday celebration wasn't even acknowledged.

The tone of my family was somber.

My grandparents were extremely attached to my son. He was the first great grandchild in the family, and he had been abducted. We had never been through anything like this. We were all devastated. We all wanted to believe that my son was still in the country, but hope was getting dim.

The next day, my older brother and I went back to my apartment. We frantically went through everything in the entire place. We didn't even know what we were looking for. I think it just made us feel like we were being proactive and doing SOMETHING. It helped keep me sane. We went through every cabinet and drawer, and even looked under the furniture. You name it, we looked in it, under it, and through it. We made it into the bedroom and started going through the dresser drawers.

My son's clothes were mostly gone. The terry cloth one-piece sleeper and T-shirt he was wearing when I last saw him were lying there. He must have changed his clothes in a hurry and tossed them. I put them in my purse to take with me back to my grandmother's house. It made me feel like I had some piece of him that I could take with me.

As we were going through the drawers in the bedroom, one of us pulled out some books and random items along with paperwork. We went through every piece. We opened one of the books and shook it with the pages facing the floor, and something fell out. It was an envelope, and on it was an address from England. We stopped and looked at each other, knowing we had just found something significant. We took everything back to my grandparents' house and decided to go back to the apartment the next day to get my clothing and personal items I needed while staying at my grandparents' house.

Back at my grandparents' house, news was awaiting us. My grandfather knew someone who worked at the airport. He called his contact and told him his great grandchild had possibly been abducted by his father. The contact told him they were not allowed to give out flight information, but in this instance, he made an exception.

It was verified through this man, that my husband had purchased a *one-way* ticket with a baby to the Gatwick airport in London, England.

It was now confirmed. He left the country. I was struck with pain so deep that indescribable sounds were coming out of me. I began pacing down the hallway, seeing myself in the reflection of the mirror at the end of the hall. I didn't know what to do with myself.

We all had suspected that was the case, but we were all holding on to some small string of hope that he was hiding out somewhere in the surrounding area, and we would have a different outcome. That string of hope had just been cut.

CHAPTER 8

The Plan

WE NEEDED TO BUY TIME. ONE OF MY FAMILY MEMbers came up with a good plan. We suspected that some of my husband's relatives were involved in the kidnapping. Therefore, I called and asked each one of them to please put Alex on the phone. I gave no indication that I thought he had left the country. Our fear was he would flee a second time if he found out that we were onto him or knew his whereabouts, and I would never see my son again.

We contacted some attorneys, and I even had an emergency meeting with a local judge to see what we could do. That was so disappointing. I felt my heart rip out of my chest when he told me there wasn't anything I could do legally because we were married.

Meanwhile, my personal prayer warrior, Nanny, was on the hotline to heaven, and so was I for that matter. That's all I could do. If I was awake, I was praying. If I was having a conversation with someone, I would pray in my mind during the pauses.

Nanny started a fast and asked us not to interrupt her while she prayed in her bedroom. (2 Samuel 12:16 NIV) She was on a mission to hear from God! She only came out of her room for a saltine cracker and a sip of black coffee to wash her medicine down every morning. A few days later, she came running out of her bedroom, praising the Lord out loud! She was in tears saying, "Monica is going to get her baby back; the Lord gave me the victory! The Lord gave me the victory!!!" (1 Corinthians 15:57 NIV)

I heard this information later that night because I was again at the apartment with my older brother. This time, there was trouble. The apartment manager met us at the door to tell us she had changed the locks per instructions of my husband, and I was not to enter for any reason. Was this happening?

I remember being outraged that I couldn't enter my own apartment to get my belongings, especially after everything else that was coming against me. It was like one betrayal after another, again and again. The punishment kept coming. I can't believe I was even functioning.

All of this was too much for me. I kept having thoughts about how devastating it would be if my child were dead, but I knew nothing. Was he alive, was he suffering, did he feel the separation from me? It was like the devil opened a portal from hell with my name on it, and things were coming at me from every direction.

I started piecing things together during all this. It was starting to make sense. Plans were being made to leave the country; it all started when I threatened to divorce him. He was planning all of this while he was out at his "counseling" sessions. The mailbox with our number on it had also been ripped out of the wall downstairs, so the mail had to be picked up at the post office. I'm sure it was done so I wouldn't see any correspondence or passport information.

One day, he even picked up the baby during a heated discussion, held him up, and smiled while whispering a song, "We are going to England." He sang it to taunt me; later, he said he was only joking. His taunting joke was now a reality and I was living the nightmare.

Meanwhile, my aunt from Florida called to talk to me. She heard that my great grandmother felt victory in prayer. She wanted to let me know that all through her life, EVERY time Nanny has ever said she got "victory" over something in prayer, it was always true— every single time—and I could trust God was going to give me my baby back.

She also said that she and I were going to agree in prayer together based on a scripture in the Bible. Jesus said, "Again I say to you that if two of you shall agree on earth concerning anything that they shall ask, it shall be done for them of my Father who is in heaven." (Matthew 18:19 KJ 2000)

My aunt then said, "The two of us are going to agree now, Monica. Do you agree?" I remember feeling so desperate as she spoke. I agreed with every fiber of my being, and I said, "Yes, I agree." Something happened after we prayed. It was now settled in me that I was going to get my baby back.

The victory prayer from Nanny and the prayer of agreement with my aunt were what I held onto. I mean I held on to them for dear life. The *how* I was going to get my baby back and *how* God planned on doing it I did not know, but my God knew.

CHAPTER 9
The Chase

THE NEXT FEW DAYS WERE A WHIRLWIND! MY AUNT from Florida called again. This is where the story gets absolutely amazing.

My aunt was a driving instructor. Every year, the driving instructors were required to take continued education classes. While at a defensive driving course, she met a private detective that helped retrieve children who had been abducted by a parent. He had a long list of credentials. It had been well over a year since she had seen him, but she would try to get in touch with him to see if he could help us.

What are the odds that you are going to run into a detective that specializes in parental child abduction and then a year later need his services? There are none! (Romans 8:28 NIV)

She ended up tracking him down through the class roster from an employee who worked at the testing site. He was living in Florida!

He said he would meet with us to see what he could do, so I booked a flight to Orlando.

The day before I left, my grandfather returned from the bank with a moneybag in his hand. He unzipped the bag, took out $20,000 in cash, and placed it on the kitchen table. He looked at me and said, "If we have to put our house up for collateral, YOU WILL get that baby back." He had tears in his eyes. I don't think I had ever seen him cry.

I was off to Florida with $20,000 strapped across my stomach in a money holder, and I was a nervous wreck. I remember flying on the plane to Orlando when the reality of all of this started sinking in.

I needed my baby. If he only knew I was desperately doing everything I could to get to him. Grief overwhelmed me at that moment, and I had to cover my face and hide. I was silently weeping. Sadness would just hit me in waves periodically. This was a nightmare, and it was really happening to me. My soul was traumatized.

I finally made it to Florida, and the look on my mom's face when I arrived at the gate to meet her is something I still remember. She was pushing back an emotional breakdown herself. We made it to her house, I got settled in, and we set up a time to meet with the detective at a local restaurant. He brought another man with him that was also experienced in this type of work. The lead detective explained to us why he would need the extra help. The house would be under 24 hour a day surveillance. The detectives would take turns watching the house day and night. It all made sense. They agreed to help us. The more I listened, the better I felt. We continued talking with them, and they shared all the options to retrieve JC, and how they thought it could be accomplished. It was the first time that I felt like I had hope in seeing JC again since he was taken.

That night, I went into the guest bedroom at my mom's house and sat down on the side of the bed. I was utterly exhausted and drained of all feelings—just numb. I sat quietly there and felt helpless and desperate. A well broke open from somewhere in my soul. There were no words, only tears and grief. It was all so much to try to process. So many thoughts and fears were constantly running through my mind. The number one fear that I couldn't allow to stay in my mind was "would I ever see my child again." That baby had never been out of my sight. He slept in the bed with me every night. I held him, and he was part of me. How can I go on? I had nothing left to say to God at that moment. I could only weep.

I silently broke down and poured my heart out to the Lord until there wasn't anything left. I was crying out to Him with tears instead of words, and somehow, I knew God was right there with me. His presence was sweet. I reached into my suitcase and pulled out

the baby sleeper that JC had been wearing the last time I saw him—
the one I found in the apartment that day. I slowly pulled it up to my
face and breathed him in over and over, I kept breathing him in.

It was him for just a moment. It was just like he was there. The
sleeper still had his scent on it, and I could smell him. It was so real.
My heart broke into a million more pieces. I buried my head in the
pillow on the bed and silently emptied out the contents of my soul. I
didn't want my mom to hear me and get upset as well. I didn't know
that I had anything left to cry, but I sure did. That moment is as
real now as it was then. I will never forget it as long as I live. (Psalm
34:18 ESV)

One of our strategy meetings was held at the main detective's house. We met his wife. They were a lovely couple. She made
us sandwiches and was a perfect host. She told me stories about
her childhood and how she just couldn't believe people in Florida
took oranges for granted. When she was a child in Germany, her
family was very poor. She remembered getting to eat an orange on
Christmas and how it was such a luxury and a privilege. She said
she kept them on hand ALWAYS. I remember she sprinkled Cajun
seasoning on my sandwich. I was glad to be talking with her while
everyone else was working out the details. She was a delight, and for
just a few moments, I almost forgot why we were there.

Our meeting was interrupted when my mom called back to Kentucky to share with my family what we were planning to do. My grandparents had been in contact with the law firm I was talking with before I left for Florida. They told the lawyers that we were planning on going to England to get JC back. The lawyers asked my grandparents to get in touch with me. They said it was urgent and for me to call right away.

I called the lawyer, and it ended up being one more crisis to endure. He very firmly urged me to stop all this foolishness, come back home, and go through the legal system. The lawyer was telling me not to trust these men. He said it was imperative that I come home immediately, so I wouldn't delay the paperwork, and they could get started on the case. He was persistent, almost rude. He kept talking about red tape and how long the process is, and that I was only delaying the inevitable. I stopped hearing the words that were coming out of his mouth. It was like white noise. He kept saying we were dragging this process out and this could tie things up even longer. I could actually feel a pull in my soul.

This was an educated lawyer telling me what I should do. I started doubting myself and the detectives. Are we crazy for doing this? Maybe I should go home and do this the right way. I should do what he said. I felt like this tension was going to kill me. I was standing there with the phone to my ear, listening to this man's opinion, while looking at the two men who could possibly make it happen. He said, "You can't trust these people. Come back, and do what is right! Sign the paperwork we need to file, so we can begin the legal process as soon as possible. We need your signature to file the paperwork, Monica." I felt guilt come upon me. Now look what I've done. We agreed to all this foolishness, and now it's going to be even longer before I see my son.

At that moment, the lead detective walked over to me and gently spoke these words, "Monica, if your son is in that country, I'm not coming back without him. I promise." It was a sign from God. The book of Isaiah says, "And your ears shall hear a word behind you, saying, 'This is the way, walk in it', when you turn to the right or when you turn to the left." (Isaiah 30:21 ESV) That settled it for me really quick. I looked into his eyes and felt peace; I knew he meant it. His wife spoke up and agreed, "If your baby is there, he will find him." I needed to believe this man, and I chose at that very moment to trust him. It was the right choice. I hung the phone up. I wasn't going back to Kentucky. This was the right way. Deep within my gut, I had to go with these men.

The next day, we drove to the Federal Building in Miami to get emergency passports. We had it all worked out. The detectives had plan A—the legal correct way of going through the court system in England—and they also had plan B, in case things didn't go the way we hoped. Plan B involved me physically removing my son from the arms of whoever had him, so that he was in my custody. I was prepared to do whatever I had to do to get him back.

We were absolutely astonished at what these men knew. They had done this before and were successful. We were going on faith, one address on an envelope, and one law through The Hague Convention that stated that my son was taken before he had the right to become a citizen. It was a law that gave us an opening to legally fight for his return. It was over a hundred years old and was still being upheld.

I believe I had been so traumatized by the betrayal of my husband taking our child that I was afraid of everyone. I wasn't completely settled about leaving the country with these two men I just met. It was strange—I knew that I should trust them, but in the back of my mind, everyone was now a potential candidate to betray me.

Little did anyone know that I settled it in my heart that when I got to England, I wasn't coming back without my son. In case plans A and B failed, I had a plan C, and it involved me staying in England.

Before we left, I shared this with my mom. I had even worked out every scenario in my head, from finding a job as a hairdresser to make a living, all the way to my last resort of survival—prostitution.

I told my mom that I would not be coming back with her if our trip was unsuccessful. I told her about my plan C. She looked at me and started crying. I'll never forget her reply. She said, "I'm not leaving without either one of you. If I have to sell my body too, I will do it; even though I may not get as much money as you would, I will do it."

When she said that, I burst into laughter. I laughed and laughed until tears started flowing. The part about not getting as much money as me, and the fact that we were talking about the most extreme ridiculous circumstances—just the thought of it sent me into one of those uncontrollable laughs that comes from deep down. I needed that laugh. She did too. (Proverbs 17:22 NIV)

Then she said, "Well...I mean it. I would do it." We laughed even harder at how ridiculous but also how serious we were. It was the first time my soul had relief since JC had been taken. Maybe the first time I smiled too.

Airfare was set up for the two detectives, my mom, and me. We boarded a plane and took our seats. It was the biggest airplane I had ever been on. My mom and I sat with the second detective as we waited for the lead detective to board. He was running late. As time went by, I started getting nervous. My mom was too. It was almost time to take off, and he still wasn't on the plane. Immediately, my mind started racing and extreme panic set in.

The second detective stood up and said, "Let me go see what's going on." He walked down the aisle and exited the plane. I knew right then and there we were being scammed. We had already paid them a portion as a retainer for this job, and now they were taking off with the retainer fee and we would never see them again. I could feel this right in my already wide-open betrayal wound. We were speechless. I didn't have the emotional capacity to handle this. How could this be happening to me? My mom and I sat in silence with fear on our faces.

Then I heard my mom say, "There they are!" I looked up, and both detectives were walking briskly toward us. The lead detective had sweat all over him. He was saying goodbye to his wife and had a bit of traffic to sit in. He had been running through the airport to catch the plane. When I saw them walking toward me, I was so relieved; it was all I could do to not break down.

Not long after that, the plane took off, and we were headed abroad.

The quickest, most economic path we could take was to fly to Germany; drive through Germany, The Netherlands, and Belgium and then get on a ferry and float over to England. Our journey had begun.

CHAPTER 10

Europe

GETTING OFF THE PLANE IN GERMANY WAS AN experience in itself. Walking into the airport was a bleak reminder of the mission we were on. Nobody in the airport was laughing or hugging when they met their parties getting off the plane. It was quiet and somber. We were far from home, and this land and people were foreign to us. The atmosphere was thick and heavy. There were German military soldiers walking around the airport with huge guns. It was a serious place to say the least.

We found a rental car place, and a young, dark-haired man in a red vest assisted us. We stood behind the lead detective, and we were getting ready to encounter our first bit of resistance. The man assisting us told us that we would not be able to rent a car. I don't remember the details why, but what I do remember is this: they were by no means going to let us rent that car. The man told us that there was nothing he could do.

I blocked out their voices, and I had a talk with the Lord. I said, "Lord, You know we need this car, and I am believing You are going to work this out for us." (Hebrews 11:1 KJV)

The next thing I knew, the man behind the counter paused, looked at the lead detective, and said, "I shouldn't be doing this, but I will." He pulled out the paperwork, we signed, and he handed us the keys to our rental car! What in the world? Instant answer to a prayer! God moved the mountain out of the way. (Matthew 17:20 NIV) He was right there with me—with us. I could sense His presence. That encounter built my faith even more and gave me the strength to go on.

Next, we drove on the Autobahn to get to Belgium. The lead detective drove and decided to take advantage of the "no-speed-limit law." We were going about 120 mph, and he pushed the gas pedal down even further. I had never been so fast in a car. It might have been fun under a different set of circumstances. When my mind tried to get a break from thinking about what we were facing, even while driving on the famous Autobahn, I was brought right back to the mission.

Every now and then, fear would start speaking to me about the fact that we only had an address to go on. The unknown was too much to bear. We had no idea if he was even at that address or if he fled to a different country. The only sure information we had was that he landed at the Gatwick airport. I couldn't let my mind keep going there.

The Netherlands and Belgium were a blur. We ate at a restaurant that was randomly positioned on the expressway. It was weird. The bathroom set up was a different too. They had stalls in the rest areas that were pay per use. I couldn't figure out the currency. They also had bathroom attendants who kept every stall sanitized after each use.

As I left the women's restroom, the lead detective asked me if I gave the attendant anything. I said no. He gave me money and told me to go back and give it to the attendant. I think he was a little embarrassed that I didn't know to leave a tip.

Drivers seemed aggressive. Traffic was at a faster pace than what I was used to, and the cars were tiny. I also recall the lead detective upsetting another driver, and the man throwing up his first two fingers at us, in a not-so-nice gesture; I knew the translation of that hand signal without needing an interpreter.

It was in Belgium that we had to catch a ferry that would take us to England. Entering the ferry on the lower deck with our car was interesting. I had never been on a boat this size. It was huge. So much was happening so fast.

The next memory I have is standing out on the deck, going across the North Sea. The skies were dreary and overcast. My mom and the detectives walked back inside, and I was standing on the deck all alone. The scene looked like something out of a movie. It was just me standing out there helpless, surrounded by unfamiliar waters. There was no land in sight, only water as far as the eye could see. I thought to myself, *Is this even real?* The magnitude of what we were doing hit me again. Sadness and self-pity wanted to consume me. I looked out across that water, and all I could see was more water. Being surrounded by those waters made me feel tiny and helpless.

I remember talking to God and telling Him how afraid I was, but at the same time, I had an overwhelming peace deep down that we were being guided by Him. (Isaiah 41:13 NIV) I stayed in constant contact with the Lord, making sure to remind Him that I was still believing in Nanny's victory and the prayer that I agreed with before I left. He was my everything on this journey.

We got off the ferry and drove straight to the address on the envelope. We were in a small village outside of London. It wasn't long before I heard the lead detective say we were close to the house. I couldn't believe it. He pointed to the house and said, "There it is."

I was looking at the house where my baby could be. I had thoughts racing through my mind. I wanted to jump out of the car and take off running toward it. My mom and I were told to crouch down low as we approached it. The detectives got a good look at it and started talking about the mission and times they would be doing surveillance on the house.

This was happening! I thought I would somehow have a bit more peace of mind being closer to my son, but that wasn't the case at all. It really just caused more anxiety. The reality of us being this close to him and something possibly going wrong was unbearable. What if we were spotted, and he takes off with JC? We would never find him.

We drove back up the road and found a small bed and breakfast (B&B) that was literally right up the street. We were so close. We signed into the B&B under false names. The detectives shared a room, and my mom and I did as well. It was a nice place. A husband and wife owned and ran the establishment. They were a lovely couple and very gracious. The detectives got settled, made sure we were OK, and then went out with night-vision gear to assess the situation and find the best areas to do surveillance on the house.

I anxiously waited for them to return with any news. The detectives came back excited to tell us they saw a red light in a window on the second floor. The lead detective said he felt really good about seeing the light because red lights are put in babies' rooms, because they are believed to be soothing. Those were words that I needed to hear. My mom and I stayed in the B&B; we weren't allowed to go outside and take a chance of being seen by JC's dad.

That night, we had dinner downstairs at the B&B. The husband, who owned the establishment, started asking us all sorts of questions while we waited for our food to be served. He started the conversation, and it was obvious that he was curious about why we hadn't left the rooms much. He asked several questions with lingering stares, hoping we would offer more information. If he only knew the truth. This would have been some juicy drama for him!

I was starting to struggle a bit with my emotions, knowing that I was so close to my child but couldn't even touch him. Every chance I had, I breathed a prayer. The biggest fear lurking in my mind was that we were chasing the wind, and he wasn't at the location we thought. That terrified me.

While the detectives took turns on night watch, I laid in bed exhausted and prayed under my breath. I had not had a decent night's sleep since my baby was taken. I cried silently, so my mom would not hear me.

The next day, the detectives asked if we liked curry, and if so, would we like some for lunch. I was tired of the food situation and must have sneered my nose up a bit about the offer of curry. He went on to say that we could also order a pizza if that sounded better. He left to let us decide. The door was almost closed, when suddenly he opened it back up and said, "By the way, we didn't see any movement from the house this morning, and there was condensation on the windows." Then he pulled the door shut.

He had no idea what he had just said. I paused for a moment of sheer joy. Condensation on the windows!!! It was beautiful music to my ears! I started jumping up and down and crying. I said, "MOM, MY BABY IS IN THAT HOUSE!!!" I kept repeating it and walking around the room like I didn't know what to do with myself. My mom was looking at me like I was losing my mind. I told her again louder, "JC IS IN THAT HOUSE!!!" I knew it for sure. God had given me a sign—just for me. (Judges 6:37 NIV) I tried to gather myself and explain it to her.

Alex would boil pots of water on the stove almost daily after JC was born. He said the humidity would be good for the baby. It used to be such an annoying thing to me because it would fog all the windows of our apartment with condensation. He was obsessive about doing this. He had all sorts of quirky habits that seemed ridiculous to me, but this one in particular stood out. Our windows were always fogged up with condensation. I KNEW HE WAS IN THAT HOUSE, BOILING WATER FOR THE BABY! As I was explaining it to my mom, I noticed the countenance of her face change. She was looking at me with a sad face. She thought I was finally losing my mind over this, and I was just grasping for straws.

I told her that it was God letting me know this, and it was FOR SURE! I frantically grabbed her by the arm and pulled her to the window. I pointed out at all of the houses and buildings and said, "LOOK MOM, LOOK AT ALL THESE HOUSES! Do you see condensation on ANY window of ANY house?"

I answered for her, "No, you don't, because they aren't boiling water for HOURS AND HOURS for a baby!" But JC's dad IS!!! I was at peace even though my mom was doubting. Why in the world would the detective feel the need to just randomly comment about condensation on the windows of the house while he was asking us about lunch? It was God working through him, and he didn't even know it.

It didn't matter to me if she understood or not, or if anyone did for that matter. I knew that my child was in that house based upon that one sentence. At this point, I didn't need to see him with my eyes to know if he was in there or not. It was settled in me that he was. How wondrous are God's ways! (Psalm 40:5 NIV)

The emotion of that day was exhausting. My mom talked to the detectives and told them about what I was saying about the condensation on the windows. The lead detective suggested that my mother go to the pharmacy across the road and try to get something for anxiety and for sleep. I knew they all thought I was on the verge of a nervous breakdown. They were so wrong. It was the first time I was actually at peace with the whereabouts of my son. But with that new information, I was even more anxious about getting JC back.

The detectives knocked on the door that evening and asked if I would like to go for a walk by the house. I was shocked. I jumped up and got ready. He gave me a zip up hooded sweatshirt and told me to pull the hood over my head. We pretended to be a couple out on an evening walk. He put my arm in his and started walking up the street. As we got closer to the house that was holding my baby hostage, thoughts were racing through my mind. I pictured myself breaking away from the detective, running to the house, and breaking JC out of there. This walk started to become burdensome.

The closer we came, the more sadness I felt. I had to gather my emotions. How in the world can I be this close to my baby and keep walking? It was torment. I held back my emotion. As we made it to the front of the house, I turned my head and studied it. I tried to take in every detail of it. I remember breathing the air in front of the house, taking it all in. But just as fast as we made it there, we passed by, and it was gone. We had to keep walking.

We made it back to the B&B. I told my mom about the walk, and we got ready for bed. I dreaded trying to sleep. My mind raced every night, and all I could do was pray. That night ended up being one that I will never forget. My mom and I experienced something that will be forever etched into our minds and hearts.

My heart was the heaviest that it had been since we started the journey. I was in my bed while my mom was getting settled. I was telling her all the details about the walk and the house. I was so exhausted. I said the words, "Oh JC, you don't even know it, but mommy is right up the road from you." And with that, I breathed a prayer, trying not to allow the sadness to overtake me. All of this was too much for me to bear. My soul was getting ready to break again and spill all over the place right in front of my mom. It was right there on the surface, but something interrupted it.

Suddenly, the atmosphere in the room changed. It physically looked and felt different. The air seemed lighter but dense, and you could see it almost like a light mist or fog—like you could touch it. It was tangible, and I could see the haze-like fog with my eyes. My mom looked over at me from across the room and said, "Wow! Can you feel that?" (Exodus 25:34-35 ESV)

"Yes," I said. Oh, I could feel it. I could see it and feel it. I had more peace in those moments than I have ever had in my entire life.

• The presence of the Holy Spirit had filled our room, and the Lord was letting me know that He was with me. "Blessed are those who mourn, for they will be comforted." (Matthew 5:4 NIV)

The Holy Spirit tangibly made His presence known to us and was right there filling the air in our room. I knew we were experiencing something supernatural and extraordinary. My soul was at rest. It was like I knew everything was going to be OK, and at that moment, I could finally sleep. My mind didn't want to go to sleep, but my body was saying goodnight in this incredible atmosphere. The Comforter was holding me. I wanted to take in every moment of this, but the invitation to rest in His presence was too great for me to resist. I whispered, "Mom, I can go to sleep now!" That night I slept like a baby. I didn't wake up to pray, worry, or stare at the ceiling. I will never forget that encounter. He is Emmanuel—God with us.

CHAPTER 11

The Highest Court

A DAY OR SO AFTER THAT, WE HAD AN APPOINT-
ment with a lawyer to petition the court for the return of my son.
The meeting was basically a question and answer session, with him
taking frantic notes. I had been prepared for this meeting by the
detectives, and it went very well. The lawyer (who is called a barrister over there) listened as I explained the behavior of my husband
and everything he did leading up to the abduction. He started calling
people into the office and giving out orders. They were taking notes
and going in and out the office. They explained they were going to
petition the High Court as an emergency case because this was an
international child abduction, and my son could be in danger.

The case was approved, and we had an emergency court date.
On the ride back, the lead detective (who was also British) explained
to me just how big of a deal this was. He said this was comparable to

the Supreme Court in the United States. He went on to talk about the history and what a big deal it was to be going there.

When we arrived at the High Court on the day of our appointment, I was astounded. It was like entering another world. The hallways were grand and had the most detailed architecture. It was enormous, and I felt humbled and very small as I walked down the halls. There was much to take in, and under different circumstances, I would have been very interested. But we were on a mission—a hurried mission.

We were shuffled into an area to wait. A small, well-dressed man with brown hair came out to meet us. He was carrying folders. He greeted us briefly, looked at me, and said, "OK, you have a little over five minutes to tell me everything. Go!"

I opened my mouth and started telling him the bullet-point version of the story to squeeze it all in. When I finished, he gently smiled at me and told us to follow him as we were going before the Judge.

Something happened when we walked up the stairs. I felt empowered. I had the most unusual strength and inner knowledge that everything was going to go in our favor. It was unlike anything I have ever experienced. It sounds crazy, but it was like I knew the outcome already. Little did I know that I was experiencing the gift of faith. (1 Corinthians 12:9 NIV)

I was being empowered by God to know and believe. I could tangibly feel His presence. It was so strong. He was WITH ME. I was caught up in this feeling, so full of faith, until we got ready to enter the door to the courtroom.

My mom looked over at me, and I could see her face—she was filled with fear. She said, "What will we do if the judge denies this?" She looked as if she could cry.

That statement was so foreign to the way I felt in my inner man that I blurted out, "I'm not listening to that. Don't say anything else if that's what you have to say." I wasn't trying to be hurtful. I just knew that those words didn't line up with the truth that was residing inside of me. I told her that what she said was not an option. She agreed. I reminded her about Nanny's victory prayer and said this is just part of the process we have to go through to get that victory. (Mark 11:23 NIV)

The lawyer told us that I would have to go in alone. My mom and detectives were instructed to wait outside. I was ready for this, and even though they couldn't go in with me, I knew I wasn't alone. It was a bit intimidating walking into that room. The judge entered, and I remembered the detective telling me that the judges were sometimes called "Lord," and in that moment, I breathed a prayer and quoted something I had heard in church as a little girl. I said, "Lord, I know you are with me whether I can feel You or not, and You are the KING of Kings and LORD of Lords." (Revelation 19:16 NIV) I was letting God know that I believed He was the ultimate judge. This was in His hands, and I trusted Him. We may have been at the High Court, but His was the Highest Court.

To tell you the truth, I was so empowered to believe we would have a victorious outcome that I actually had to make my facial expressions look serious, like I had concern. My lawyer, whom I only talked with for mere moments, stood up and gave the most incredible argument I have ever seen. It was like this man had been with us through the entire journey. My jaw wanted to fall on the floor. He was AMAZING. He flawlessly and very urgently petitioned the court for the return of my son. It was like he was born to do what he was doing. God didn't line up just any barrister for me. He had the very best.

The judge asked why the child shouldn't stay here with his father. I was praying. I said to Lord, "I don't care what's coming out of his mouth right now. I have the victory."

The lawyer's responses were astounding! He was fighting for my son like it was his very own child. He was unstoppable! And victory is what we received. The judge granted a motion for the immediate removal of JC, and if needed, they would do it by force!

We went back to the B&B. The detectives went to the house to watch everything unfold. THIS WAS HAPPENING NOW! When they arrived at the location, the police were there as well. The detectives looked nervous for the first time. This was out of all our hands. I remember looking in the eyes of the lead detective before they left. I didn't have words, and he didn't either. Both of them were silent.

As soon as they made it to the location, they called me on a cell phone they left for me. The lead detective described every detail of what was going on. The police were there and had surrounded the house. He said neighbors were coming out of their homes, wondering what was going on. A small crowd was gathering.

The owner of the B&B couldn't help himself any longer and just came right out and asked us what was going on. It was almost a relief to tell him. My mom shared why we were there, what our real names were, and all the details up to what was happening at that very moment. His eyes were wide as he listened. He and his wife were now part of this with us and were a corner of support while the drama unfolded.

I was listening to the detective. He told me that the police had the place surrounded and were knocking at the front door. This went on for several minutes with no response. I was hanging on to every breath that came out of his mouth through that phone. He told me that they were bringing a door ram to open the door by force. My heart was racing. "Wait," the detective shouted, "The door is opening! The police are going in!"

Within two minutes, I heard the greatest words I have ever heard. He said, "I am RIGHT NOW watching them bring your son out!!! I AM LOOKING AT YOUR BABY RIGHT NOW!!!!!!"

As I repeated the good news, the floodgates opened. We were all crying, even the owners of the B&B. After about 10 minutes or so, the detectives made it back to the B&B. When they came in, I could see both of them had been emotional because their eyes were red. When the lead detective looked at me, a couple of tears welled up and fell down his cheeks. I grabbed him and cried and then grabbed the other one. We didn't celebrate long because the police had JC at the station, and we needed to go there to get him.

The next thing I knew, we were on our way to the police station to get my son. I will never forget walking up the concrete sidewalk. The police department had a glass door, and as I walked closer, I could see someone inside. I recognized who I was looking at. It was Alex! I wish I could tell you that with all the praying and talking to God I had been doing, I responded like a good little Christian girl, but that wasn't the case. What fell out of my mouth when I saw him was a slur of words that were not Christian, or anything that even closely resembled Christian words.

I had so much anger when I saw him. I felt like I could physically attack him. It had to be the Holy Spirit that reminded me of what my great grandmother said when she took me into that room to pray after JC was kidnapped. I heard the words "Be humble." (Micah 6:8 NIV) And I also heard the detective tell me that I needed to calm down before we entered.

They made me wait outside and went to tell the police I was there. The officer told us that Alex had arrived ahead of us, and they had just taken him into another room. He had no idea that we were in the country! He thought we did all of this by phone. He was trying to convince the police this was all just a big misunderstanding. He told them his wife knew he was in England for a holiday with his son, and this was all just a mistake.

They took me straight to the back room where some officers were holding JC. My eyes saw him. I had to touch him. I went over and picked him up. He was wearing a dingy white terry cloth sleeper, and his diaper was wet. I made sure I was gentle. I had rehearsed this moment over and over in my mind. I wanted to make sure that I was in control of my emotions so as not to scare JC. I slowly reached for him as the female police officer gently handed him over. Not a dry eye in the house. I felt like I would never be able to put him down again. I finally had him. I could breathe. He was in my arms. This nightmare was almost over.

Since plan A seemed to be working out, we continued down the legal path. We had one last court appointment at the High Court. Alex would be there this time.

The lead detective was also a military veteran, so he set up accommodations for us to stay at a place called The Union Jack Club in London. It was for the military and their families.

We said our goodbyes to the owners of the B&B, drove to London, and got settled in at the military club. It felt safe, and I was grateful. Honestly, there couldn't have been a better place for us to stay after getting JC back.

The first thing we did was give him a bath. We noticed at the police station that he had a terrible diaper rash. That bath was symbolic for me. It was so much more than getting him clean—it was washing away the abduction. After we got him ready for bed, we were completely exhausted from the events of the day. I was a little disappointed that JC wasn't making the same eye connection or smiling at me like he did before he was abducted. It hurt my heart, but it wasn't long before he was smiling and connecting with me again. I slept in the bed with my baby boy that night and even shared him with my mom.

That next day was filled with activity. We had to find a store that had baby formula, diapers, and all the other things we would need for the remainder of our time in England. The detectives took us to downtown London for a shopping adventure. We found all the baby items we needed and so much more! WHAT AN EXPERIENCE!

I needed to purchase something to wear to court the next day. The streets of London were so busy. It was like a different world. We did a bit of sightseeing in between shopping and saw several of the things that you would want to see if traveling to London. As we went about the day, we ended up visiting Harrods, a famous store in London, where we were told that they guarantee to find almost anything you need (it'll cost you, of course).

It was a time filler for me; I just wanted to go home. I didn't care if I ever saw this place again. Maybe one day, I would be interested in coming back, but for now, this place was beyond an inconvenience to me. It had too much pain associated with it.

That day, two people downtown passed out while walking. People were rudely stepping over them to get where they needed to be. The first person was probably just dehydrated or overheated. The second person who fell was actually having a heart attack.

We witnessed something that day that the detective said would make the papers and may never happen again. The man who had the heart attack needed to be airlifted. A medical helicopter flew over us and had to successfully maneuver itself between all the buildings and people. We didn't know what was happening until it was over. For several minutes, as we watched a helicopter invade the city, fear struck us all as we thought London was under some sort of attack. I remember thinking, *Surely, this can't be happening to us after everything we've gone through!* How much more can I take?

After all the excitement of that day, we made it back to The Union Jack Club. We had dinner there and then went to our rooms. The next day would be action packed.

We woke up and got ready for our appointment at the High Court. The plan was to have my mom stay at the hotel with JC. If for some reason, the judge didn't rule in our favor, we were going to call her and have her take off to the US Embassy with JC, and we would meet her there. We were not leaving the country without him.

I left for the High Court once again. When I entered the courtroom, Alex was already there. The process went quickly, and everything went in my favor, granting me the right to take my son home.

We left the High Court and wasted no time. Phone calls were made, airline tickets purchased, and we started the process of going home. We needed to get an emergency passport for JC, so we went to the US Embassy. We were trying to time this, so we would make our flights at the Gatwick airport.

We were all on overdrive! Everything we did was fast! After getting JC's passport, we took off for the airport in a cab. The detectives took care of everything we needed, from figuring out the currency when purchasing something to making sure that we didn't get ripped off by cab drivers, or anyone else for that matter. The lead detective told me that in some cases, cab drivers would take longer routes when they knew they had a tourist in the car, so that they could get the extra fare. It almost happened to us in the cab, but the lead detective knew where we were, and he instructed the cab driver to take us in another direction. These men were handpicked by God to help us.

The lead detective was the mastermind. He told us he chose the other detective not only to help with surveillance, but in case we had to implement plan B. He was just as important and would be the muscle man in case we had to physically take JC back.

I am grateful that plan A worked out, and I am forever grateful for the gift these men gave me. I could never repay them. I hope to see them both again one day and introduce them to a grown-up JC and the rest of my family. I completely lost contact with them.

It was a mad rush to the airport. We called the airline to tell them we had a child who had been retrieved from an international abduction that would be boarding the plane. When we arrived, the lead detective grabbed JC's car seat with him in it, and we took off running. We were all sweating and exhausted, but it was good exhaustion!

I was on my way HOME, and I was the happiest I had been in a very long time! The happiness was short-lived because when we finally made it to check-in for the flight, we were met with bad news. The customer service person said, "I'm sorry, that plane is preparing for flight."

What did she mean by "Sorry"? Sorry wasn't acceptable. We went on to explain that we called in advance to let them know the circumstances about the abduction. The customer service agent made a phone call. She then informed us that the plane had pulled away from the walkway but was still there. Surely, they can back up five feet and let us board, right? Wrong. The lady told us that we would have to make other arrangements.

My mom had taken all the emotional pain of this trip; she was strong and kept her head together—that is up until this point. She opened her mouth, and out came an entire international child abduction worth of emotion. The service agent would receive the brunt of it. She said, "AFTER ALL WE'VE BEEN THROUGH, YOU CAN'T HOLD THIS PLANE LONG ENOUGH FOR US TO BOARD? WE CALLED IN ADVANCE AND WERE TOLD YOU WOULD HELP ACCOMMODATE US BASED ON THE CIRCUMSTANCES! I AM GOING TO SUE THIS AIRLINE!!!"

The lead detective gently pulled her aside and tried talking to the agent. My mother was sobbing at this point. She just couldn't hold it together any longer. We booked new flights, and all waited together at the airport. The detectives booked flights to their destination, and we booked flights back to Kentucky.

It worked out better that way because we ended up getting to say proper goodbyes. We had been in a whirlwind since the journey began, so it was nice to have that time together. We took some photos with the detectives, talked, and decompressed from all that had just happened.

When it was time for them to catch their plane, I had a moment of grief come over me. We had been through so much together. They helped me get my child back. Would I ever see them again? Is this it? After all that we had been through together, it was finished now. I felt a bit of a loss. They hugged us, and we all had watery eyes. We said our goodbyes and waited for our boarding time. Finally, they called us to board, and we walked on to the plane to find our seats.

My mom found her seat but mine ended up being at the other end of the plane. We asked the attendant if there were two seats together. She said no. My mom explained the situation. The flight attendant immediately walked over to the intercom telephone hanging on the wall.

She said, "These two women are returning home from an international child abduction. Is there anyone who would give up seating arrangements so they could sit together to tend to this child?"

It went completely silent, and then it seemed like every hand on the entire plane went up in the air. People were shuffled around, and we were seated together. Once we were seated, everyone on the plane started clapping. We were shocked at the response.

As the plane took off, the older gentleman who was sitting closest to me eventually started asking questions, so I told him what happened. His eyes filled with tears by the end of the story.

Finally, we were on the way home. Everything seemed to be fine during the flight until JC started vomiting. He kept vomiting repeatedly, and we thought it might be serious.

After everything we had endured, what was one more thing? We were becoming experts at dealing with drama. Even though I wasn't shocked that something else was happening, I was afraid. My nerves had been traumatized and were maxed out. I felt rage toward

Alex again for putting this little baby through all of this. We were supposed to have a brief layover and change planes in Atlanta, but we decided to take JC to a hospital during that layover instead.

We were SO close to being home! When we stepped off the plane in Atlanta, I realized what people felt like when they kissed the ground after coming home from a long journey. It felt so good to be back in America. Even if it wasn't home, I was grateful beyond measure to be back in the United States.

We went to a children's hospital in Atlanta and had JC checked out. He had altitude sickness and would be fine. One more flight to get home. We were way past exhaustion from this journey. We made it back to the airport and boarded our final plane home.

When we arrived at my grandmother's house, everyone was in tears. JC was passed around for everyone to hold. We sat down and told them all about our journey. It felt so good to be home. The nightmare was finally over, and I could rest. The rest was nice, but would be very short-lived. One week later, JC's dad was back in the United States. Another battle was just beginning. The divorce/custody battle was on the horizon. That battle became a sixteen-year war.

CHAPTER 12
Letting Go

MY GREAT GRANDMOTHER, NANNY, DIED WHILE ALL of this was happening. Before she passed, she told me that she knew the Lord kept her alive, as long as He did, to pray JC home from London.

It would be months before I would leave the house to go anywhere without JC. I had some serious anxiety and post-traumatic stress issues from the ordeal. I was awarded full custody of JC and his dad walked away with a scolding from the judge, and supervised visits, with the stipulation that I choose the supervisor.

I was hoping that the judge would lock him up and throw away the key, but I didn't get so lucky. The judge told him that if the two of us hadn't been married, he would have sent him to jail for the abduction. Since we were married when it happened, his hands were tied.

Alex would not accept the ruling of the court. It would be his way or no way. For five years, he fought tooth and nail for the visits to be unsupervised. He could not accept supervised visits. He dominated me verbally and tried to control me with intimidation, manipulation, and threats throughout the entire process.

We battled it out in court until JC was 16 years old. He made my life a living hell, but to tell you the truth, it made me stronger. The Lord was using this experience to teach me Dominion. At one point, He even pressed it upon my heart to pray for JC's dad. This started another process of forgiveness and healing where I learned to forgive and try to keep my heart free from offense. Oh boy, did I have plenty of opportunities to practice.

On one of the many occasions of him sending the police to my house, I decided I had enough. The police knocked on my door. I opened it, and they questioned me about why my son wasn't allowed to go on his court order visit with his father. This was absurd.

JC was now 16. He already talked to his dad and told him he was sick and wouldn't be going on the visit. Changes were not allowed; plans could not be altered with this man.

I told the officer that JC wouldn't be going with him today because he was sick, and his father knew about this. He questioned me further and informed me that if I was interfering in the exchange, I could be arrested and charged with custodial interference.

I don't know why, but this day was different. I looked the officer straight in the eye and said, "Do what you have to do." I wasn't going to be intimidated or bullied ever again. If I went to jail that day, SO BE IT!

I decided if I did in fact go to jail, I would tell every woman in jail about Jesus and lead as many people as I could to Him. I would just look at it like a mini mission's trip—I was not going to be moved!

The police officer talked to JC and went back outside to tell Alex that JC was indeed sick, and did not feel like going with him. He went into a fit of rage in front of my house. He even became aggressive and threatened the officer, in an attempt to force the visitation. The officer came close to arresting him.

After it was over, he sent me a threatening email telling me that I would see him in court. His phone calls, meetings, and correspondence usually consisted of me being called filthy names that I wouldn't put on paper. Several times, it even happened in front of JC.

My husband Dave had never interfered with JC and his dad at any time, but when I told him about all the new drama and the threatening email, he responded with wisdom. He simply asked, "Why do you let this man hold power over you?" Those words were a confirmation to what was already in me.

- I would not respond to Alex ever again. He could take me to court, email, call, or send police to my door. It didn't matter. I was finished; I had enough.

I recognized that I had been giving power away and was being pushed around because I felt like I had to put up with it. It was another lesson in Dominion—getting my life back from someone that had Dominion over me, just like the Lord spoke to me that day as I was driving down the interstate. I could keep this cycle of crazy drama going or end it. I chose to end it. I was equipped now to know that life didn't just need to happen to me; I could make decisions to help decide the outcomes of my life. It was one of the greatest decisions I ever made.

When I finally drew the line in the sand, the world didn't end, I wasn't thrown into jail, and my son wasn't taken away. In fact, every irrational fear pertaining to my ex-husband, which held me hostage, came to an end as well. Little by little, with God's help, I was taking back every area of my life that had been stolen from me. He was restoring everything the locust and canker worm had eaten. (Joel 2:25 KJV)

I was learning Dominion.

CHAPTER 13

The Knight in Shining Armor

AFTER THE ABDUCTION, I WAS CONSUMED WITH fear and even paranoia. I was afraid JC would be snatched out of my arms. I was afraid his father was going to break into the house at night and take him again. I stayed with my grandparents after I came back to the States with JC.

Everyone was afraid. It was a traumatic event for my entire family. They had an alarm system installed soon after I moved in, but it didn't stop the fear. It was months before I would leave the house without him. People would periodically call to see how I was doing and ask if I wanted to hang out, but I wouldn't leave my son.

After some convincing from my family that I needed to get out of the house, I reluctantly went out with a friend. She said we should go to a local bar that had live music and dancing. We went, and I had a good time. It felt good to be out in public and take my mind off everything.

As the night was ending, I ran into someone I dated in high school. Since our dates then revolved around him and his friends looking for whatever high they were pursuing, things quickly fizzled out.

He acted thrilled to see me and wanted to get my number. We started talking and realized that he lived only a few streets away from where I was staying at my grandparents.

He was a breath of fresh air after everything I had just been through. He was great with my son and confided in me that he couldn't have children. He said if things worked out with us, he could see us getting married and adopting JC (be still, my broken and still bleeding heart…,). I couldn't resist this knight in shining armor who was here to rescue me and put the broken pieces back together.

Maybe I would have a real family after all. We dated for several months, and he eventually got tired of visiting at my grandparents'. He talked me into getting an apartment with him. We found one and moved in together.

It wasn't long before I became pregnant. He was really excited that I was pregnant (but wait, I thought he said he couldn't have kids). Even his mom told me that it was a good thing that I already had a son because he couldn't have kids. Nevertheless, I put that thought aside. I was happy that he was happy, and I felt like my life was finally going to start taking a turn for the better. The only other problem I had was my family was not OK with what they called "shacking up," and that is what we were doing. How was I going to tell them that I was pregnant and not married?

The reality hit me that not only was I pregnant but I was also still legally married to JC's dad. The divorce was long and drawn out due to the abduction. To make matters worse, my attorney informed me that I could not get a divorce while being pregnant.

As the pregnancy progressed, my knight in shining armor decided that he was going to start going out with friends after work. He started coming home later and later every night until one night when he didn't come home till the sun came up. I was so hurt. I couldn't believe this was going south too. What was wrong with me? I just could not take it anymore, and I moved back into my grandparents' house.

After a couple of months, I noticed the knight's truck going down the street to a house across from my grandparents' place. I couldn't believe what I was seeing. He was parked at a house where a single mom lived with her parents. He and I met her months earlier at a party she was having at that very house. Yes, it just kept getting worse.

As the days went on, his truck stayed longer and longer until it was parked there overnight. He eventually moved in with them, and I had a front row seat to the event. I could look out the front window of my grandparents' living room and see it all. This was happening at the time I found out we were having a baby girl.

One day, I was walking by the living room window, and I saw him on a riding lawn mower with her little girl on his lap while he cut the grass. There I was pregnant with this man's baby, and I could look out the front window of the house and watch him play daddy to someone else's child. It absolutely crushed me. The rejection and abandonment wound was ripped wide open. It was the straw that broke the camel's back. What was wrong with me? I must not be good enough. How could this be happening to me? I was in the middle of a divorce and pregnant with another man's child, who had now started cheating on me with a girl down the street.

In the beginning, he lied about their relationship when I confronted him. He was still stringing me along, but the truth is he had already moved on. His family was quiet about it and pretended to not know what was going on. But now, he was almost flaunting it right out in the open. I was so ashamed that I fell for all his lies and promises. I felt like an idiot. How will I explain this to everyone?

I knew he had addiction issues with drugs and alcohol back in high school. When we moved in together, I started watching him go deeper into the addictive behaviors, but again, my need to be loved and accepted by someone was stronger than any sign or warning.

My mom was still living in Florida. I called her and told her everything that was happening. I was so broken and honestly didn't know what to do. I couldn't fix this. She wanted me to go there and stay with her, and I did. I packed up my things and left for Florida, completely broken.

The new environment was nice. I could breathe there. As I look back, I was running away from the shame of my situation, more than anything else. It was so good not knowing anyone or feeling like I needed to explain anything about myself. I stayed there until my daughter was due and gave birth to her at a local hospital.

She was beyond beautiful. Tiny little thing with a full head of dark hair. When they put her into my arms to feed her that first night, I looked at her and just broke. I loved her so much. I would do anything for her. I remember looking at her and thinking that without a half of a second of hesitancy, I would jump in front of a bus and end my life to save hers. I held her and fed her and thought she was worth anything and everything that I went through up to that point. She was my girl.

My mom brought JC to see us the next day. We sat JC up in the hospital bed with us and let him get to know his baby sister. He was so excited. It was a special time for all of us.

I had an awesome "God thing" happen before I left the hospital. I thought long and hard for months about her name and decided it would be Jenna. I wanted her name to be special. I wanted it to be something different, but not too different, so I wanted to be sure it felt right. Most importantly, I wanted her to like it.

The hospital administration person had been by to see me several times. She couldn't file the paperwork for my girl's birth records without her entire name. I was still missing her middle name. I went back and forth and over the long list in my mind but just could not decide. I told the administrator that I would make a decision for sure the next day.

That night as I was feeding her, the name McKae just dropped into my mind. I loved it and thought it was perfect!!! Jenna McKae! She was born on St Patrick's Day, March 17. McKae even sounded Irish! I loved it. I picked up the phone next to my hospital bed to call my mom and tell her about the name. I dialed the number and got a busy signal, which was odd. So I hung up, and when I did, my hospital phone rang. It was my mom. She was so excited. She told me she was trying to call me, but the line was busy. She blurted out, "I have a middle name—what do you think of McKae?" I was SPEECHLESS!

She kept talking; she said she was watching a movie on television and saw that name roll up on the screen during the credits! It was spelled differently but pronounced the same. I was almost shouting with excitement! I said, "That's the same name I was trying to call YOU with!" She couldn't believe it! I couldn't either! Did that just happen? There was no way it was a coincidence. We knew that was supposed to be her middle name. It was settled!

I know God was giving us something special about her birth and letting me know that even though her natural father wasn't involved, He was. He was with her. He would NEVER leave us or forsake us. He was giving her a special gift. She would hear that story and know that she was planned to walk on this earth. (Psalm 139:13 NET) He knew the vehicles that would be used to get her here. He knew the circumstances she would be brought into. He not only knew her but he named her.

She's grown now. She turned out to be a beautiful, gifted human being. She is an artist and an amazing singer, and she has a way and love for animals like no other. I love her so much and am so grateful that she came into my life.

CHAPTER 14
Coming to Jesus

FLORIDA WAS A PLACE OF REFUGE FOR ME, BUT I was starting to get homesick. I ended up going back to Kentucky shortly after my daughter was born. My mom eventually moved back to Kentucky as well. By that time, I was trying to piece my life back together. With a loan from my grandfather, I opened a small hair salon with a business partner. My mom and I also moved into a two-family home together; she had the upstairs, and the kids and I had the downstairs. Things briefly looked like they were getting better for me, but that wasn't the case at all.

The salon was great, and it could have been a lucrative business except for a few problems. I was secretly diving deeper into a cocaine addiction, while my business partner had some struggles of her own. We eventually parted ways, and I closed the salon.

Addiction became a top priority for me now, and I was starting to scare myself with some of the choices I was making. I was lying to my family all the time to cover my drug escapades.

One time stands out above all the others. I was trying to get my daily fix from one of my drug dealers. After reaching him, we set up a time to meet. There was only one problem. I didn't have anyone to watch my son.

At this point, all the bridges were burned for childcare with my family. I lied to them too many times. I would tell them that I would be back in a couple hours, but one thing would lead to another, and while chasing a high, I would break my promises.

Because my son had been abducted when he was a baby, I would only allow family to watch my kids. This day, I was in a pickle. I ended up desperate to get what I needed and ended up bringing my son along for the ride.

This was a huge compromise for me. I had some sense of self-righteous goodness that believed "I'm a good mom because I don't take my kids around my drug dealers." Wow, I know…insanity, right? When you are at the bottom of the pond, you'll look for anything to make you feel good.

I was driving down the road with my son in his car seat. I remember having the thought that I could quit this stuff if I really wanted. I also remember thinking that I didn't want to find out if that was true. I parked the car in front of the drug dealer's apartment. I tried calling him to get him to come outside, but he couldn't. I was starting to panic. I can't just leave him in the car to buy drugs, but that is exactly what I did. I locked him in and took off in a mad dash to get my fix. While in his apartment, I stood by the window watching my car. I kept telling him to hurry up.

The entire transaction took about three minutes, but those three minutes were enough to pull the string of the entangled ball of mess that I was.

I drove away and thought, *If I did this, what would I do next? What kind of mom takes her kid on a drug deal? Maybe I can't quit this stuff…Maybe I am addicted….* Things just got worse from there.

I would stay up for days at a time and sleep late into the day. My family was starting to get fed up. I was running out of excuses, and my addiction was spiraling out of control. My life was past being unmanageable. I finally told my grandparents that I had been taking pain pills, and it had gotten out of hand. There was no way I could tell them it was cocaine.

This cycle continued and I was stuck. I couldn't function or start my day without cocaine. I was tired. The best coke around was never enough. My nasal cavities were destroyed. I was really thin, to the point that my pants would fall off without a belt (I thought I looked good). I was having random nosebleeds at the most inopportune times and places. I needed help.

Around this time, I was introduced to the man who would become husband number three. He was charming, a real smooth talker. He was talented and the number one sales person in his company. He owned a nice home and seemed like a great guy. He swept me right off my drug-addicted feet. He liked to party too, so we hit it off! It was perfect timing because I needed to be rescued, and this man seemed like just the lifesaver I needed.

A lot happened during my third marriage. It was bad on top of bad that eventually helped me bottom out. We would separate for weeks, get back together, and repeat that cycle over and over. It was during this relationship that I surrendered to Jesus.

During one of our times of separation, I was at my grandparents' house. It was about 5:00 am, and I was coming down from a three-day cocaine binge with no sleep. I could feel my body shutting down. It needed rest. I laid down on my grandmother's couch and tried to close my eyes, but my eyes were not cooperating with me. Every time I tried to shut them, they popped right back open. My heart was pounding in my chest so hard that it seemed like I could hear it. I was afraid I could possibly have a heart attack. I was too high. It might have been the first time that I had ever felt that way. I was scared.

At that moment, the thought came to me that I could not keep living like this. I wanted out. I was tired. Without even hesitating, I found myself crying out loud as I wept. "God, if you are real, please get me off this stuff!"

The words pressed out of me like they had been waiting to come out for a very long time. I meant every word with every fiber of my being. I was crying out for help. I don't know why I said "if You are real"; I knew He was real. I knew the God that saved me as a kid, the God who was with me when my son was abducted, the God I saw move through people in church services…that God was real; I just needed to find Him again, if He would have me that is. I needed HIM to rescue me. I needed Him. "Come to me, all who are weary and heavy-laden, and I will give you rest." (Matthew 11:28 NASB)

After I cried out, nothing miraculous happened immediately, but something was happening behind the scenes.

Several days later, I got a phone call from my younger brother. I recall him talking to me and shooting straight from the hip. The conversation went something like this, "Monica, I'm not sure what you've got going on in your life right now, but you really need to get a job. I have a friend who works at a salon. I talked to her about you. She said they need hairdressers, and if you just show up for the interview, she is sure they will hire you. You are good at what you do; I think you should check it out." He gave me the contact information and told me to give them a call. I waited a few days and called the number. The man on the phone wanted to meet me right away. I set up a time a time to meet him and waited.

When the interview day came, I was getting ready in the bathroom, and there was a problem. I needed to get high and I knew I couldn't go to the interview in that state. But I really needed it. Against my better judgment, I snorted a little bit, just so I could function. I didn't think anyone could detect that small of an amount.

Well, I wish I could tell you that I had that kind of self-control, but I didn't. I ended up doing almost a gram of cocaine before that interview. I was as high as a kite and not coming down any time soon. I went to the interview and tried to not look the owner directly in the eyes for long periods of time. I only remember him showing me around the salon and smiling at me a lot. He hired me, gave me a start date, and I was now working in the salon.

Husband number three and I got back together, and I thought maybe this time, things would work out.

I liked working in the salon. The owner and his wife were great to work for. I smoked cigarettes at the time and cussed like a sailor.

I took breaks in the back of the building with some of the girls. I was getting to know everyone, and things seemed to be falling right into place. I did notice some odd things that started happening to me there.

I noticed that I was the only girl in the salon with a potty mouth. I started making an effort to watch what was coming out of my mouth. It also seemed like every other person who sat in my chair had something to say about the Bible, Jesus, or their church.

One day, I had my hair dryer on high while styling a woman's hair. She started chatting with me, but I couldn't really hear everything she was saying. I was only catching bits and pieces over the noise of my hairdryer. I was trying to read her lips through the mirror so I didn't miss everything she was saying, but I also wanted to get her hair finished and take a break from standing on my feet.

She was animated and enthusiastic. She used her hands a lot while she talked. I heard her say that she was putting together a Bible study for a group of people at her church. I could tell she was super excited about this project. She said she was making a shield and looking for a sword that she could use for a prop, because she was going to knight each person at the Bible study.

At that moment, a cool breeze hit me and chills were all over my body. Every hair on my body was standing at attention. It was like an unusual awareness came over me in slow motion.

Why are all these people talking to me about Jesus? It's happening WAY too much to be a coincidence. I mean it was so often that it was like neon lights flashing on and off, trying to get my attention.

Then, I heard a gentle voice inside me say, "You asked me if I was real." It was at that moment that I knew that the God of my childhood was trying to get my attention. He was answering my prayer and showing me that He was real. There was no way this was an accident!

The owner of the salon had been inviting me to his church repeatedly, so I figured I should go that weekend. But instead of going to the church, I went to a campground with some of my party friends. I brought an eight ball of cocaine and was sitting at a tiny kitchen table of the camper, breaking it up to divide out lines to snort. I couldn't get all this Jesus stuff out of my mind. I knew I should have gone to the church, and I was feeling a little guilty. I decided that the next weekend, I would be there for sure.

There I was cutting up cocaine with a credit card and thinking about Jesus. I told the people I was with that I was getting ready to let God turn my life around. As I said those words, it seemed like a fog came in the camper, and the atmosphere changed. It was the same fog that came into the room when I was in England! I don't know how to describe it exactly, but it was like peace and warm liquid love. A billowy presence enveloped us.

Everything seemed lighter. One of the ladies had fallen away from her relationship with God. She knew what was happening. She asked, "Do you feel that presence?" I shook my head yes, and then she said very seriously, "That is the presence of God." She said, "I may not be living right, but I know that presence."

"Where can I go from Your Spirit? Or where can I flee from Your presence? If I ascend to heaven, You are there; if I make my bed in Sheol, behold, You are there." (Psalm 139:7-8 NASB)

We were silent and still for a moment, and then I lowered my head and snorted the line of cocaine in front of me. My days of bowing my head to drugs were about to be replaced with bowing before The King of Kings.

I ended up meeting my boss and his wife at their church the next weekend. I don't remember anything about the service that day, except for waiting for the invitation at the end. The pastor asked anyone who wanted to turn their life over to Jesus and invite Him into their heart to pray. That was what I was waiting for. I was so tired of struggling to live my life without Him. I needed Him. I knew I was going to surrender. I prayed along with the pastor and meant it with all my heart. I couldn't keep living my life like this. I just knew this was the thing I was supposed to be doing.

That week as I was driving to work, I was giggling to myself. I realized that I had been led to a Christian hair salon and none of this stuff happening to me was by accident. I was listening to my new favorite Christian radio station, thinking about how it seemed that all the events that had been happening to me were orchestrated by God. I was thanking Him for coming into my life. I kept feeling goosebumps and was smiling from ear to ear.

I can remember the exact stretch of the road that I was driving on when the realization hit me that I hadn't had one thought or craving for cocaine. I used to taste it in my mouth when I needed more or had gone too long without it. I realized that the taste for it wasn't there anymore. I knew darkness had been removed from me, and it was gone forever. The addiction was spiritual darkness, and it wasn't inside me anymore. Jesus had removed it and set me free. "Therefore if the Son makes you free, you shall be free indeed." (John 8:36 NKJV)

At that very moment, I started weeping and thanking Him out loud, and when I did, liquid love enveloped me and flooded my soul. I cried even harder. I just kept thinking that He took the addiction away from me FOR FREE, and I knew I was never going back. I told Him right there that I would go wherever He wanted me to go, do anything He wanted me to do, and say anything He wanted me to say. I was diving all the way in. I felt so good, and so brand new, that if I didn't share this new life with people, I might explode.

Sometime shortly after that, I walked past the bedroom mirror on my dresser and glanced at myself. I was stopped dead in my tracks. I had to do a double take. My face looked different. For real. Something was different. I looked softer, or at peace in my countenance. I felt good—lighter, better. I even had a thought that I liked what I looked like. That had never happened!

I went to work, and my boss said, "Wow, look at you!" I smiled so big as he asked me why I looked so good and what was different. I told him that I had given my life over to God. I kept giggling like a lovesick teenager and couldn't stop smiling. He told me that my face actually looked different. I knew exactly what he was talking about, because I saw it for myself. I had Love living inside me, and it was spilling out to overflow; I couldn't contain it.

I've heard lots of other testimonies about people getting saved; some don't feel anything, some do. I felt brand spanking new. It was like my eyes had a hazy film removed off them or passed through some windshield wipers, and I could see clearer and brighter. Colors were more vibrant. Darkness had been occupying me, and Jesus made it leave.

I felt love for people that I didn't have before. Suddenly, I just knew that they were precious—even people that weren't so nice to me. It was all so real. I passed from death to life. I was a new creature in Christ. (2 Corinthians 5:17 NIV) This was something that I could not deny.

I wanted to know everything about God. I wanted to know Him. I felt like I was alive for the first time in my life, and I was never turning back. God was real, and His Spirit was living inside me—and I knew it. I would never be the same. Everything was good, well almost everything…

CHAPTER 15
Husband #3

NOW THAT I HAD THE LORD, I HOPED HUSBAND number three would get on board as well. This was the missing piece; surely, he would see his need for Him too.

I started praying and asking God for a miraculous turnaround for my marriage. The harder I prayed, the worse things seemed to get. The closer I moved toward God, the further my husband moved away.

I continued to plead with God to do something. Then one day, I said, "Lord, I've asked you for so long, and You see the way this man treats me. When are you going to change him?"

I heard that voice speak again, and this time, He simply said, "I'm going to change YOU!"

If I could put my feelings at that moment in a picture form, I probably looked a whole lot like a dog when he tilts his head over slightly and ponders like he doesn't understand.

"Huh? Change me? Why in the world would You need to change me? That doesn't even make sense. I'm the one living right, going to church, and doing all the things a good Christian is supposed to do. Why would You need to change me?" I can imagine the Lord smiling and getting a good chuckle at that one.

This marriage was looking like another failure. I just didn't understand. "What's the matter with me, Lord? What am I doing wrong?"

What I didn't know then was that God wanted to do an inside work on my soul—surgery to the wounds of my past. He wanted to transform me from the inside and heal my mind. (Romans 12:2 NIV) He wanted me to take my life back instead of my life ruling over me. God wanted me to have healthy relationships, and that was happening, except in the area of men. I was holding onto to that one part of my life with white-knuckled fists, but I didn't know it. It was an area of my life that was not surrendered to Him—my need to be loved.

It's funny now that I know the truth. I believed somehow that God was responsible for the way my life was going. At this point, I was totally oblivious to the fact that I was the one making all the broken choices. I would make a choice, and when it didn't work out, I would question God as to why He kept letting this happen to me.

I was the one choosing the broken people. I just didn't understand why yet, but He did. He knew how I was going to choose, and He was using every broken choice to give me a new understanding and get me back up on my feet. It was the beginning of the turning point in my life.

God taught me a powerful lesson through this marriage. His will is always to heal and restore, but He cannot override a person's free will. We can pray for someone until the cows come home, and we can be sure that God is dealing with them, but ultimately, it's up to that person to respond.

We must agree with His will, and the work He wants to do in us or through us. (Philippians 2:13 NIV) I wanted God to give me a miraculous turnaround and heal this marriage. I kept asking Him, pleading with Him to do something, but He wasn't talking to me about the marriage. He *was* speaking to me, but it was about another subject matter.

God began to reveal more things He had for me. One day, I was walking across my living room, and I heard the words, "I am going to use you in the healing and deliverance ministry." I knew it was God! I loved that he had just spoken to me, and I was excited about healing. But I wanted to push that deliverance word right out of my mind, and that's just what I did. Healing is miraculous and beautiful, but the word deliverance has something to do with demons. (Matthew 10:8 NIV) I wanted no part of that.

One weekend, I bought a box of books at a yard sale. They were all Christian books, and the price was one I couldn't pass up. The one on top was about the Song of Solomon. It was what I had been studying at the time, so I was thrilled! I brought the box home, opened the book, and tried to dig in. I was excited to learn more, but the book seemed flat, and I couldn't get into it.

I set it aside and picked up the next book in the box. It was called *Blood on the Doorposts: An Advanced Course in Spiritual Warfare* by William Schnoebelen. When I read the title, I knew this wasn't an accident. I was supposed to read this book, but I didn't want to. I was afraid of demons. I had been tormented my entire life by them. I knew they were real because sometimes I saw them, felt them, and on occasion, even smelled them.

They invaded my dreams on an off throughout my life. I wanted no part of this, none whatsoever. I had a little talk with Jesus. I said, "Lord, I will do this healing thing, but I'm not doing any of this deliverance stuff." I heard nothing back.

A few days passed, and curiosity got the best of me. I opened the book and started reading. Oh boy, this stuff was intense, and I didn't like it. I made myself read through it but only with the lights on. I was uneasy about it, but I knew it was something I was supposed to be doing.

I started throwing myself into learning as much as possible on the subject. There were spiritual forces opposing us in this marriage, and I also felt like the Lord had been showing me that my husband needed deliverance. The more I learned about the subject, the more obvious it was that the spiritual was impacting the natural.

Around that time, a fight escalated with my husband, and I feared that it would get violent.

I felt this was as good a time as any to try out this deliverance stuff. I walked up to him, looked him in the face as we argued, and I said these words: "I am not speaking to you; I am speaking to that legion of demons inside of you, and I am telling you that you are leaving!"

Without any hesitation, a voice from another world came out of his mouth and answered me back saying, "NO, WE ARE NOT!"

Every hair on my body stood up, and I could feel something on a spiritual level that I had never felt. It was like every cell in my being was on alert—I was in total shock. That sound coming out of him was not his voice. I wish I could tell you that I stood my ground and made the demons leave, but after that encounter, I didn't care if they left or not, because I was leaving! I got out of there as fast as I could!!!

What in the world? Did that just happen? Yes, it did happen, and things like that were about to start happening to me more and more.

We went to counseling as a last-ditch effort. We had a few meetings with my pastor and were given steps to bring restoration, but my husband wouldn't go any further. He didn't want to surrender and chose to continue the same destructive behaviors.

God will intervene if we allow Him, but like I said, we also must be willing. He was not willing.

After praying for months concerning how I should respond in this marriage, one day the Lord simply spoke a scripture into my heart. I looked it up, and it said, "Can two walk together, unless they are agreed?" (Amos 3:3 NKJV) He was answering my prayer, but not in the way I wanted him to. I wanted Him to tell me exactly what to do, but He didn't. He only asked me a question. I answered the question. Two cannot walk together unless they are agreed.

I told my husband I wanted a divorce, and he filed the paperwork about a week after that. It was a long messy process that took well over a year.

CHAPTER 16

The Projects

I ATTENDED A FEW PRAYER MEETINGS WITH A GIRL from work. She was following Jesus too, so we hung out quite a bit. The meetings were OK but kind of boring. The attendees sat around, listening to worship music and prayed a lot. I started to think that these types of meetings were not for me.

These people sat in their chairs or laid on the floor, praying for the entire meeting. My mind would wander all over the place. I was thinking how this prayer stuff just wasn't my thing. Well, not yet anyway…

One night as we were leaving, the guy leading the prayer group said he asked God to only bring those people that night who would be connected to their ministry. Oh, did I ever show up on the wrong night! I wanted to sneak out before he finished speaking. Afterward, he asked me if I would be able to meet with him and his wife the next day. I agreed but was perplexed.

I met with them the next day, and they asked me what I thought about the group. I told them that I liked everyone and it seemed like a good group. After some small talk, he told me the reason they had asked to meet.

He said, "We feel like God spoke to us and said you are going to lead our healing and deliverance ministry."

I could have fallen off my chair. Speechless. My mind was blown!!! It was a confirmation of what God said to me in my living room that day! I never mentioned that to anyone.

I became great friends with these people and loved them like family. His wife became a best friend. She helped me get on my feet, as I was recovering from the divorce. She set up a meeting with the manager of an apartment complex nearby.

The manager gave us a tour of an apartment, and I was not impressed. My friend said this would be perfect because it was so close to her house, and if I ever needed anything, they could be there to help me out. I reluctantly signed up for the apartment and was approved.

The kids and I moved in. I just couldn't believe that this was where God wanted me. The apartment was a mess. It was supposedly freshly painted but clearly was not. The smell of nicotine and semi-yellow walls was proof that it had only been spot-painted. The carpet was bad, and the padding was broken down. I didn't even want my kids playing on it.

One night after we were settled in and the kids were asleep, I had a serious talk with the Lord. I told Him that this was NOT BLESSED. There is no way that He could have sent me to THIS place to live. I broke down and cried. I went on and on to Him about the condition of the apartment and how I was afraid to even let my kids go outside to play here. I felt so let down. I fell asleep on the couch that night, crying.

The apartment had so many issues that I was now on a first name basis with the maintenance man. I had to call him repeatedly about issue after issue. At some point in a conversation we had during one of his repair calls, he asked what I did for a living, and I told him that I was a cosmetologist. He perked up and seemed REALLY interested in this and asked me if I would be willing to meet his wife. I said yes, and he went outside to call her. He told me that his wife's hairdresser seemed to have dropped off the face of the earth, and she was desperately seeking a good colorist. Color just happened to be my specialty. Within the hour, his wife walked from the other end of the complex and introduced herself.

The maintenance man's wife and I hit it off. She scheduled a hair appointment with me immediately, and before long, I had her for a loyal customer. In a very short time, she also told all her sisters about me. I would go to their apartment to do their hair, or they would come to mine.

During one of the appointments, one of the sisters asked me what I did for fun and where I went to party. This conversation led to me telling them my story and how I didn't really "go out" anymore as it pertained to clubs or nightlife. I told them how The Lord supernaturally set me free from cocaine addiction. I told them about Jesus and how He changed my life.

When the conversation shifted to this subject, I had the full attention of everyone in that room. It seemed like time stood still as I shared with them. I felt a calmness come in the room, and you could hear a pin drop. The hair all over my body was standing up as I talked to them, and they kept making comments about getting chills. As I went on with my story, I noticed a couple of them were crying.

After that day, everything changed. These girls wanted to know anything and everything I knew about God and how they could get Him for themselves. One by one, each girl eventually gave her life over to Christ and became sold out. They had joy and peace like they had never known.

During this period, I had a vision. As I walked down the stairs of my apartment, I saw chairs going all the way around the perimeter of my living room. I couldn't explain it or what it meant at the time but saw it very clearly and thought it was significant. (Joel 2:28 NIV)

Soon after, these girls wanted to get together in a group to learn more about Jesus. A friend recommended I borrow some chairs from church that were reserved for this very thing. They delivered them to my place, and the next thing I knew, we were having a bible study/ prayer group in the living room of my apartment.

As I walked down the stairs one morning and glanced at all the chairs lined around my living room, I realized it was exactly like I saw in the vision that day, except it was in real life.

Wow! I could see how God was showing me that He was with me and that He was working behind the scenes in all of this. These girls were just like me—broken but hungry to be saved and changed by the only One who could do it.

They were getting set free from drug addiction and emotional pain, and even getting filled with the Spirit. It was amazing to watch and especially to be a part of. The freedom in Christ that was given to me was being given to them. (Matthew 10:8 NIV) We were all on the same team and the same path, I had just traveled a bit further up the road and was sharing with them what I knew so far. They wanted more, more, and more. The power and presence of God met with us every time we got together. He was with us.

"For where two or three are gathered in my name, there I am with them." (Matthew 18:20 NIV)

One morning, I went to meet a couple of the sisters. When I arrived at the apartment, they let me in, and all I can say is that I'll never forget what happened next. The older sister needed to talk with me, so we went upstairs into a bedroom where she shut the door. The other sister was downstairs. The two of them had been on the fence about Jesus, and this day would be the day they made their decision. It wouldn't come without a fight…

The younger sister started pouring her heart out about guilt and shame from her past. She didn't think she could be forgiven of the things she had done. I told her that she was the perfect candidate for His love and that He knew everything about her and everything she's ever done, and nothing was too bad for Him to forgive—NOTHING.

She was weeping at this point and started confessing what she had held in for years. This stuff had her in shackles that you couldn't see with your eyes, but they were there nonetheless. I told her about how she could be saved and forgiven. I told her how Jesus was punished and crucified, and paid the penalty for all our sins so that we could all be forgiven. (Romans 4:25 NIV) I asked her if she wanted to pray with me and receive Him. She said yes.

As soon as we started to pray, we heard a loud noise like something had crashed into the wall downstairs. It shocked her and caused her to stop praying. I sensed that it was a distraction from the enemy and told her that there were dark forces that didn't want her to come to Christ. I told her to ignore it and keep moving forward.

"For we do not wrestle against flesh and blood, but against principalities, against powers, against the rulers of the darkness of this age, against spiritual hosts of wickedness in the heavenly places." (Ephesians 6:12 NKJV)

We could hear a man's angry voice downstairs, screaming obscenities. It sounded like he was throwing things against the wall. I had a strong sense to push forward.

We finished praying and walked downstairs to see what all the commotion was about. It was the oldest sister! Her face was beet red, and that angry man's voice that we heard was coming out of her. She was shouting curse words nonstop and throwing things. I walked right up to her and started talking to her. I asked her if I could pray with her as well. She shook her head yes but was still shouting obscenities at me very loudly. She was pacing back and forth like she really wanted to hit me. I could feel the intimidation.

The voice she spoke with sent chills through every fiber of my being. She followed me upstairs, and I asked her if she wanted to give her life to Jesus. She shook her head yes. I explained what was happening to her.

I told her that we have an enemy of our soul and that she was being influenced by an enemy spirit that was trying to keep her from turning her life over to God. I shared with her that the moment her sister started to pray was the exact time she started yelling and throwing things. This was seriously intense.

I could feel the direction of the Holy Spirit. I told her I would lead her in a prayer. We started to pray, and I asked her to repeat after me. She opened her mouth to speak, but nothing came out. She was grabbing her neck and opening her mouth trying to get a sound out, but still nothing. I knew it was an evil spirit in her keeping her from speaking.

I felt an empowerment and strength come upon me, almost like a helium balloon just expanded in my stomach that was full of boldness and authority. Out loud, I said, "This woman has agreed to pray for salvation through Jesus, and you have to take your grip off her. I command you to let go of her mouth RIGHT NOW, so she can speak in the name of Jesus!" Instantly, she let out a big gasp and could talk.

She started crying and looking at me like she was questioning what was going on. I assured her that everything was OK and we just needed to pray. I explained to her that the enemy had her in his grip and had rights to her because she wasn't saved. (Colossians 1:13 AMP) I directed her again to repeat what I said and to do it with all her heart to the Lord. She asked God to forgive her for all the sins that she committed in her life and invited Jesus to come into her heart and be the Lord of her life. I then said a prayer over her. I asked her if she wanted to be filled to overflow with His Spirit. She said yes. I started praying and asked the Holy Spirit to fill her up from head to toe.

The whole atmosphere changed as the presence of God filled the room. You could physically see peace come into her.

"And the peace of God, which transcends all understanding, will guard your hearts and your minds in Christ Jesus." (Philippians 4:7 NIV)

Even her facial expression changed; the lines on her forehead softened, and she was gently weeping in the presence of God. She touched her long hair and said she felt so good. She just wept in the presence of her new Savior.

That moment was unforgettable. She looked like a young girl who was in love. She was glowing. That same girl was screaming obscenities with a different voice just moments before. It was a beautiful thing to be a part of, but also a terrifying experience. We have a powerful God that can set us free!

When I left there, I was so worn out. I was asking myself if that really just happened. I was blown away. I went home to rest from the ordeal and to process the whole thing.

The encounter I had with the sisters was different from the encounter with my ex-husband. I was equipped and ready this time. Now don't get me wrong, I was afraid when it happened, even shaking, but I was empowered by the Spirit of God as to what to do and what to say. I felt like when I spoke, whatever was there had to listen and do what I said. It was authority from God. I had power over that darkness, and I knew it. (Luke 10:19 KJV)

I started thanking God for what had just happened. He set the whole thing up somehow and used ME to get His will accomplished for their lives. The pieces were starting to come together.

When I made it home, I fell into a heap of brokenness. I was exhausted and elated. I was His. The Lord God ALMIGHTY was with me, living inside me, and working through me. I knew it like I had never known it before. I was in absolute awe of what God was doing in that low-income apartment complex and how he was using me to help these girls get to know Him.

Then I remembered the night when I laid on that exact same spot and how ashamed I was to live there. I had told God there was NO WAY that He could have led me there and had told Him that this was NOT BLESSED.

I was so humbled and a little ashamed for not trusting Him. I told Him I was sorry and that I could see it now. Sharing Christ and getting to be a part of helping these women get free was one of the greatest blessings I had received as a Christian. Make no mistake about it; I was EXACTLY where God wanted me to be. He brought me there, and it WAS blessed!

I remained heavily involved with my prayer group and tried to never missed a meeting. I read every healing and deliverance book that I could find. Some things were unfolding beautifully, while some made me want to run away and never look back.

But it was too late for me. I had seen too much, and I knew all of this was from the Lord. My eyes were open, and I was all in.

CHAPTER 17

The Bike

THE KIDS AND I WERE ADJUSTING TO LIFE AT THE apartment complex. They were doing great in school, and my daughter was set to be honored in an awards ceremony. They were giving recognition for things like character, attendance, and good grades. I was doing everything I could to keep my head above water while managing life. I was going to college and working with the prayer ministry in my spare time.

I fell short of being the mom who showed up in class with the homemade chocolate chip cookies or volunteered to chaperone at school outings. Instead, I was the one who was always in a rush and not looking forward to losing the time, when I had so many other things to do. I usually grumbled to myself before events like this but always enjoyed them after I got there.

It was held in the gymnasium. The stage behind the podium was filled with rows of tables filled with prizes for the kids. There were water guns, board games, puzzles, dolls, and a range of other prizes for each age bracket.

In front and center of the prize table was a bicycle that was obviously reserved as a special grand prize. The announcer called out each child's name, and one by one, they walked up to the announcer, shook hands, and received their certificate. Then they were directed to the rows of prize tables where they could shop and pick out any toy they wanted. It was a pretty cool idea, and you could tell the kids loved it. As you could imagine, this took quite a bit of time because choosing a toy is important business to a kid.

As the announcer continued, at least half of the toys were missing from the tables when my daughter's name was called. She got her certificate, walked to the tables, and picked out the toy that stood out to her.

This process went on for some time when something strange happened. A young girl's name was called, and what she did has made a mark on me since that very day.

This small girl in a sundress walked up to the podium, shook hands, and got her certificate. She turned around and walked directly to the bike that was on the front row, grabbed the handlebars, and started rolling it back toward her seat.

You could almost hear a pin drop in that place, except for the gasps of people concerned and even embarrassed for the little girl.

She was walking off with the grand prize!

Something even more strange happened after that. They called out another child's name, and the event continued. They didn't go after the girl to collect the bike or put it back. They didn't redirect her to the table to pick out a lesser prize.

That bike was just one of the prizes that was up for grabs, and any child who wanted it could have walked up to it and rolled it away as their prize.

I was shocked. We all just assumed that the bike was a special prize reserved for a special winner. My head was spinning. I thought to myself how many times in life did I settle for the lesser thing because I didn't feel worthy of the good prize. I had chosen the lesser all too many times, whether it be friends, romantic relationships, or just about anything else. I ended up choosing people and making choices that reflected the way I felt about myself—unworthy, not good enough. I would have never walked up on that stage and taken the bike. It wasn't even an option.

The event was over, and I drove home and had a serious talk with God. The bike thing had me completely undone. A new perspective was on the horizon, along with a shift in my thinking. That bike represented so much more than an elementary school prize. It represented how little my thinking was and how I felt about myself.

The knife cut deep that day, but it was being cut with the hand of a specialist, a skilled surgeon, the Great Physician. The One who made me and could see my brokenness. He was asking if I would let Him do surgery on my soul; He was the only One qualified to operate.

He was with me and wanted to restore me. He wanted me to feel like the girl that knew she was worthy of her bike. That little girl in the sundress didn't have a thought about not being worthy of that prize. She had something that I didn't, and I wanted it. I didn't care what it cost.

"I say yes to the surgery, Lord." Tears streamed down my face, and all I could say was "I want the bike Lord, I want the bike." I felt heaviness and emotional pain from realizing that I had settled for less my entire life.

The pain I felt was real. I wanted to change. And I mean, everything. Especially the way I thought. I wanted to be the girl that gets the bike. Help me to see the way you see, Lord, not small-minded or not good enough. Help me to renew my mind.

The greatest Teacher that ever walked the earth was walking with me. He was going to help me get my life back and restore me to my rightful place.

"But you are a chosen generation, a royal priesthood, a holy nation, His own special people, that you may proclaim the praises of Him who called you out of darkness into His marvelous light." (1 Peter 2:9 NKJV)

CHAPTER 18
Husband #4

MARRIAGE NUMBER 4 WAS THE HARDEST AND greatest lesson of my life. After this mountain, I would never again be able to tolerate not being valued in a relationship. I lost a good portion of my hair through the stress, and it just about killed me. But I believe it was designed to do just that.

A good friend introduced us one night at the prayer ministry. She was related to him. She told me of his broken past and how he had gotten radically saved. He too had been addicted to drugs and was now sold out to Jesus.

He had a great testimony, and he knew the Bible. We had some conversations, and he seemed like a great guy. We got to know each other during ministry functions. We began seeing each other more and eventually started dating. It was nice to date a real Christian and to have conversations about God. I was so impressed with how much he knew of the Bible.

One night, he shared with us that he was awaiting a court date for something from his past. He said he was ready to face whatever happened, even if it meant going to jail. He asked if we could all pray for him, and we all gathered around him to pray. While we prayed, I thought how sad it was that this bright and shiny new Christian could end up doing time for something in his past. It seemed so unfair that he had finally got his life together and now he might go to jail.

His court date came, and he was sentenced to serve time in jail. He spent almost a year there. Several of us wrote to him and went to visit him. It was obvious God was with him. He was learning and growing and had gotten connected to the chaplain. People were being led to Christ, and it seemed that the Lord was using his situation for His good.

He wrote to me every week while he was in jail and eventually started disclosing very serious feelings for me, hoping that when all of this was past him, we could pursue a future together. I was flattered but also felt like it was crazy for me to have feelings for someone in jail.

I also thought that things were going well while we dated, and I couldn't hold this thing from his past against him. We continued to write to each other while I was working and going to college full time, trying to make a better life for myself and the kids and move out of the low-income housing.

As time went on, I started thinking more and more about this man. He was a real Christian, and he was actively pursuing me at this point…finally, a real Christian.

I thought that with our similar backgrounds, we would be an awesome witness to the saving power of God, and who knows; maybe God was bringing us together for ministry to help people who have been on drugs.

He asked me if I would ever consider marrying him, and shortly after he had been released, I did just that. My kids were so happy; they really liked him, and we were looking forward to getting a real house and becoming a family.

I knew early on that it was a mistake. I started seeking the Lord because I realized that I had gotten myself into another mess. I received confirmation when the Holy Spirit spoke these words to me, "If you asked me for bread, would I give you a stone?" (Matthew 7:9-11 NKJV)

Everything went south very fast. This man's true colors were coming to the surface as he started opposing everything I did, especially prayer. He didn't want me to pray, and it got to the point that he didn't even want me to speak. I mean, things became very dark. I felt like I had been TOTALLY DECIEVED. This can't be happening to me again. What am I going to do now? I was so ashamed. Now what? I'm stuck for the rest of life because nobody will ever marry me again if this doesn't work out.

This was my fourth marriage and my second marriage as a Christian.

This time I recognized that it wasn't God that brought him into my life; I did. I chose it...and God being God knew how I would choose and was going to use this situation—every drop of it—and did He ever!

There was physical and verbal abuse and even an attempted suicide right in front of my very eyes. I was so stressed out from this marriage that my hair started falling out. I developed stress-induced asthma. I just could not go through another divorce as a Christian. I had to try to keep the marriage together. I couldn't handle the shame of another divorce.

I was doing ministry work now and living in two different worlds. Life would seem fine for a couple of weeks or even a month and then radically shift into chaos and strife that would not let up. There were holes in my walls and doors.

Now that I knew about deliverance, I started interceding heavily for him. I tried everything in the world to make the relationship work or at least hold it together until God moved. I was walking around on eggshells, absolutely devastated.

We tried counseling, psychologists, deliverance prayer with ministers. Some of it seemed to work, but it was always short-lived. He would get angry and throw things across the room, and a couple of times, full soda cans were thrown at my head. He threatened to burn the house down and he eventually fell back into addiction.

One day, a disagreement turned violent, and before I knew it, his hands were wrapped around my neck and he started squeezing. I looked in his eyes with shock that he was doing this to me. When our eyes locked, I saw a wild look in his, and I was terrified.

All the sudden both of his hands INSTANTLY flew off my neck with a force that made them come off as quickly as they landed. He looked shocked and then ran out of the house. To this day, I believe an angel came to my rescue and removed his hands from my neck.

"For He shall give His angels charge over you, to keep you in all your ways. In their hands they shall bear you up, Lest you dash your foot against a stone." (Psalm 91:11-12 NKJV)

After the choking episode, I had to separate from him and get a restraining order through the court. I had to have peace.

The whole ball of yarn was unraveling.

I made an appointment with the psychologist we had been seeing. My husband refused to keep seeing him, and I wanted to fill him in on what was happening.

I wanted desperately to get to the root of my issues and to understand why I kept getting into such a mess.

CHAPTER 19

Courage to Change

THE DAY I WENT TO COURT FOR THE RESTRAINING order was a life-changing day. I was stressed out from the event. After it was over, my mom came over to show support and talk with me. She wanted to take me to lunch and clear my mind from everything that was happening. We chose a local family restaurant.

Once settled inside, I noticed a small group of people in light-blue polo shirts. One woman stood out. She looked over and smiled at me. I couldn't help noticing throughout our lunch that the lady was glancing over and smiling at me periodically. She had the most genuine smile.

We finished eating, paid for our food, and walked outside to leave. The group in the blue shirts was standing around a car that just so happened to be parked next to mine. We had to walk around them to get to our vehicle. I was getting ready to open my car door when the little lady with the beautiful smile turned to say hello. She was staring at me with that smile again.

She asked me if I wanted to know why she kept looking at me. I stared back, and before I could answer her, she said the Lord told her that I was His daughter. He told her that I was going through something very difficult right now and that I needed to be encouraged. God also told her to tell me that He loved me and was going to bring me through the situation. The words she spoke refreshed me and brought hope to my soul! (Proverbs 25:11 KJV)

She walked over to her trunk, popped it open, pulled out a book, and handed it to me. It was a book she had written called *Stopping the Cycle of Self Abuse*. She told me to read it. My mom and I stood there with our mouths wide open. God showed up in the parking lot.

The lady walked over and gave me a big hug. After the embrace, I noticed the logo on her shirt. It was a jail ministry logo. My eyes widened, and I said, "I just recently asked someone if they knew how I could get involved in jail ministry!" A very tall silver-haired man looked up and said, "Lady, it is no accident that we are meeting today." He pulled out a business card. He was one of the founders of the ministry. He told me to come to a meeting the next weekend.

Soon after that, I was going to the local jails, telling my testimony and seeing lives changed right before my very eyes! Girls were getting saved and delivered. It was powerful and life-changing for me. I knew God had a purpose for me despite all my mess.

Meeting those people was not a coincidence. It was a mile marker of destiny and strength for my journey.

I devoured the book the woman gave me. When I finished reading it, I contacted her. I learned that she was the founder of a ministry that helps women. She asked me to go for a ride to see the ministry. She took me on a tour of the three-phase complex, and within a couple of weeks, I was working for her.

It was a transitional living program for women. Most of them were trying to find their way out of addiction. Some came right off the streets or out of jail. The name of the program was "Having the Courage to Change." I smiled when I found out the name.

I knew I wasn't just there to help those women have courage. I was there for change, too. God wasn't going to bring me to a place with a name like that and not ask me to change.

My marriage was falling apart, but God was restoring my soul. It was there that I realized how truly broken I was. I saw it in the women going through the program, and I recognized it in me. They didn't know who they were. They didn't value themselves.

I prayed standing at the front door of the ministry after finding out the name of the program and said, "I say yes Lord, I want the courage to change. I'm scared of what that might mean, but I want it."

I loved working there. I cooked meals for them, handed out medicine, and walked them to their apartments. I facilitated small groups and Bible studies. I felt a supernatural love for these ladies and saw the power of God show up mightily in their lives. I watched some of them change and grow. I heard stories that ripped my heart out a thousand times after hearing what some of them had suffered. The abuse they were exposed to at the hand of others was horrifying. Often, while driving home from work, I would be overcome with a burden to pray for them.

During a morning shift, I was facilitating a group. There was a new woman who had arrived the previous day. She was African American, tall, and very quiet. She didn't speak a word throughout the entire meeting. I shared my testimony with the girls and talked about how the Lord set me free from drug addiction. She listened intently but had a look on her face like she did not care for me or about what I had to say. After others shared and we talked a bit, she walked up to me and asked if she could meet me privately when I had time.

I took her downstairs into the office where we administered medicine. It was policy to lock the door when handing out medicine for privacy issues. We went in, and out of habit, I locked the deadbolt.

She started talking immediately and told me the story of how she used to be a good Christian and that her husband and children still go to church. She fell into addiction and started using heroin. She was living on the streets and doing anything to get the drug. She said she was desperate for God to help her. When she heard my story, she thought maybe I could pray for her.

During the prayer, I noticed she began crying, and I reached out for her hand. We were both sitting in chairs facing each other. I bowed my head to pray and had the words "Spirit of Fear" come into my mind. I ignored it and tried to continue praying, but the words just kept coming to my mind.

Ugh, I was trying to pray for a simple, little God help and bless her prayer; I really didn't want to hear about a Spirit of Fear. I felt an intensity in the atmosphere, and the words kept coming.

Before I made the decision to say it in my mind, my mouth began speaking the words "Spirit of Fear." By the time, I made it to the word "fear," her head shot back, and she started shrieking and screaming in terror. She ran backward to get away from me, jumped up on a chair, and started clawing at the wall like trying to climb up it. It was like she was completely terrified of being near me.

An intense feeling of intimidation suddenly hit me. I was physically shaking. All I could do was think about how to get out of the room. The deadbolt was locked, and I was stuck with a demonized woman manifesting; it literally felt like she wanted to kill me.

I realized I needed to get myself together and remembered I had authority. (2 Timothy:1-7 NKJV)

It was like a helium balloon started filling up in my stomach area, and I felt empowered. My flesh was still shaking, but I moved toward her anyway. I grabbed her hands while she was still shrieking and said, "Spirit of fear, GO in the name of Jesus."

She seemed to deflate right in front of my eyes. She let out a sigh and fell into a heap. She was back to herself and crying. She shook her head back and forth in disbelief. She looked up at me and asked, "How did you know, how did you know? Isn't it just like God to use a WHITE LADY…" She kept shaking her head, "Isn't that just like God to use a white lady?"

She went on to tell me that her mom had been murdered by a white woman, and she has had hatred for them since. She said she didn't want to listen to me talk during the group, but as the meeting went on, she felt a strong urge to ask me for prayer.

She repeated the question again, "How did you know?" I said, "I didn't know anything until I heard the Holy Spirit speak the words 'Spirit of Fear.'" She smiled, shook her head again, and said, "Isn't that just like God..."

She asked to hug me, and when we embraced, she broke again and just sobbed. I loved her from that moment on. The barriers had been removed, and that woman loved me too.

Many amazing things happened during the short time I worked there that I will never forget. I hold those memories and those women dear to my heart. Being part of that ministry and watching those amazing women overcome obstacles was another mile marker on my journey to dominion and inspired me to have the Courage to Change.

CHAPTER 20

Roots

MY HUSBAND AND I WERE STILL SEPARATED, AND the restraining order was still in effect. It looked like the marriage was coming to an end, and at this point, I secretly hoped for it. A tiny part of me held on to the fact that God could intervene and bring change. But the change wasn't happening in the marriage; it was happening in me. It was all becoming clearer.

I woke up one Sunday morning and had a thought pop into my mind about visiting a church I heard about through some friends. It was about 35 minutes away from where I lived. I thought it would be a breath of fresh air and nice to not have anyone from my regular church, asking questions about what was going on in my marriage.

I made it on time to the service and sat way at the back. The worship service was awesome, and it felt good to be somewhere nobody knew me.

During the end of the music, someone got up and took the microphone. They said they felt like the Lord wanted us all to pray for marriages.

UGH…That was the last thing I wanted to do. I told the Lord that I didn't want to pray for my marriage anymore, but if He wanted me to pray for others, I would. I reluctantly bowed my head along with the entire church as we started praying out loud for marriages. I was discouraged and thought that I surely picked the wrong day to visit this church.

I glanced up front and saw that one of the leaders seemed to be looking at me, and then she started pointing at me, repeatedly. I was one of a few Caucasian folks there that day, so I felt like I stood out a little, even though I was seated at the back of the church. I looked all around to see if she was possibly (hopefully) looking and pointing at someone else, but she wasn't. She was pointing at me. She came down the aisle almost running at me and pointing her finger. When she got to the end of my pew, she started motioning her hand for me to come toward her. I walked over, and she leaned over into my ear and spoke these words: "God told me to tell you that whatsoever you choose, He will honor, because you have found favor in the sight of God. He said whatsoever **YOU CHOOSE**, He will honor…"

It was what my soul had been longing to hear. I started crying and dropped my head. The dam that had been holding back all the pressure broke open, and I was free. Wow! I sat there in awe of God and thanked him for answering my prayers. I knew I was released from my marriage.

Later, I called that church and made an appointment with the woman pointing at me. She was the associate pastor there and an amazing woman of God.

I told her everything that I was going through—all of it. When I was finished, I asked her what she thought. She took a long pause and said, "I'll tell you what I think...It sounds like you need to get out before he kills you." I was so shocked from her statement. She said, "Honey, the church will tell people to stay in foolishness! God never calls us to be abused." I needed to hear what she was speaking.

I went home that night and was processing everything that had just happened. I was thinking about all the embarrassment and shame I had, especially pertaining to divorce in the church. And rightfully so, divorce is the subject of controversy and is more than frowned upon. (Malachi 2:16 NASB)

I had several Christians tell me how God hates divorce, but I was coming to the realization that God hated His daughter being abused even more than He hated divorce.

For so long, I tried to do the "right thing" as a Christian to keep my marriage together, in hopes that God might break in and heal it.

But what if there was more? Maybe I was putting up with this type of behavior because deep down, I was afraid of being alone... This thought stopped me dead in my tracks, and I asked the Lord, "Am I hiding behind Christianity and staying in an abusive marriage because I am afraid of being alone?" Maybe down at the root, there's more.

A huge lightbulb went off in my mind. It would be the lightbulb that set off a chain reaction that would bring about a lasting change in my life. I needed to heal and find who I was, apart from anyone else. I filed for divorce.

CHAPTER 21

Melon Thumping

I FELT THE NEED TO LAY DOWN MY DESIRE TO HAVE a romantic relationship. I knew it was necessary if I wanted to be whole. The old saying goes that when the student is ready, the teacher appears. Things I needed to know and the people sent to help me started showing up.

The next two years were a turning point and a time of restoration. I learned things about myself and the way I view the world based on my experiences. I discovered that fear of abandonment and fear of rejection caused me to act out and make wrong decisions, that would in turn cause me to repeat broken cycles again and again. I learned about my strengths and weaknesses, and oh boy, were there weaknesses—insecurities, vulnerabilities, and control issues rooted in fear! It was time to identify these old ways of behavior, let them go, and find new ways to cope.

I took some intense classes on codependency and dug up old wounds that needed healing. I went through deliverance and inner healing ministry. This was like an open-heart surgery of my soul. The Great Physician was at work in me. (Mark 2:17 NKJV)

I didn't want to bring any more old baggage to another relationship. I didn't want to keep getting the same man in a different body, and I didn't want to settle ever again for less than God's best. I'd rather be alone; in fact, being alone started feeling good, and I started liking myself. I was at peace with me and loving this new place God was leading me to.

I went to a psychologist for a while and made good progress. His name was Dr. Taylor, the same psychologist that provided counseling during my last marriage. I took away so much from this gifted man of God. Every time I left his office, I felt better.

Eventually, he told me that I did not need to schedule any more appointments. On our last appointment, he asked me a scary question. He said, "Monica, do you really want to know what's wrong with you?" I was a little startled by that question. My heart skipped a beat, and I looked him right in the eyes; "Yes" was all I said, but I felt like looking away and sticking my fingers in my ears to keep from hearing the damage that could be coming.

He said, "Nothing, nothing is wrong with you. You just jump into relations too soon without doing your homework. You are an attractive woman, so healthy normal men as well as crazy men are attracted to you.

"There are differences that can be seen in both *if* given enough time. Crazy usually can't hide for longer than a few months. It will eventually start creeping out. Most anyone can be on good behavior for are a few months, but when you have spent enough time with someone, you will eventually see who they really are. Crazy people are usually impulsive, and they get to you FIRST, and because you haven't given it enough time, or done your homework, it ends badly.

"Normal healthy men have some distinctive traits about them, and when you know what to look for, it will help you to decide if this man should be a friend or if you should move on. Notice that I said *friend*. I want you to start fishing for friends.

"Think about when you are making plans with friends. You go places with them. You meet out for lunch or do fun things together. You would never curl up with a friend on your couch late at night and make out...because you are friends! Friends do friendly things. I want you to start fishing for male friends.

"It's during this time that you will be watching and learning. When you have gotten really good at this, you will eventually see who is becoming a best friend. When you find your best friend, that's who you should consider marrying." (Matthew 7:20 NKJV)

"Have you ever thumped a melon? You need to learn how to thump a good melon. My wife knows how to thump a good melon. When you are shopping for melons, there is a certain sound that you can hear when you thump it. They even have a certain smell. There are distinctive traits to look for to see if it's ripe and of good quality."

"I'm going to give you specific traits to look for to help you find good friends. You are going to find out how they respond to the word 'no' or what happens if you change plans suddenly. How do they respond? How do they treat their mother? Do they have many friends, and if so, how long have they had those friends? Do they work? How long have they worked there?"

The list went on, and I listened with everything in me. I was so ready for this. Everything in me was ready for change.

Oh, if only I could have had this information years ago!!! It would have helped me so much! He said that when I find my best friend, if I am still concerned, I should schedule an appointment, and he would be happy to evaluate him for me!

This had us both smiling. With my track record, it probably wasn't a bad idea; so I made a mental note of that one! I made up my mind that I would take this new information and apply it. It was the first time in my life I felt equipped for relationships.

It wasn't too long before I would get to put some of my friend-fishing skills to practice. A friend introduced me to someone. We went out and had fun. I was armed with new skills and feeling confident about applying them. My heart had been through surgery, and I had come out on the other side. I was in no way looking to jump into another relationship, and for the first time in my life, I was completely satisfied and even enjoying being by myself. I felt like I was in a good place to try this friend-fishing thing out.

This guy seemed like he met most of the requirements on my list from Dr. Taylor. He had all his finances in order and even had what seemed like some bonuses. He had faithful, lifelong friends and a family that loved him. He held Bible studies once a week in his basement, attended church, and even went on mission trips. After a couple of months, he was very upfront and told me his intentions. Things seemed to be going well, but my heart just wasn't settled.

By this time, I was working for an employment education program as a teacher and life coach. I taught classes on interviewing, branding, resumes, and even codependency. One of my favorite classes helped people overcome in some of the same areas that I had struggled. It was an amazing feeling to see people set free.

One afternoon, a text message came through my phone from the guy I had been dating. It said that he would like to start looking for engagement rings. When I read it, I gasped out loud! I wasn't expecting that.

There was someone who had been quietly painting my office for a few days. He stopped working and asked if everything was OK. I laughed and told him that I thought the person I was dating was sort of proposing to me through a text message!

This was getting serious, and it was something I needed to hear from Heaven about. I had been through too much. There was way too much at stake now.

That weekend, I started asking the Lord to confirm things about him. I really liked him, but there seemed to be something missing. I laughed out loud in my car and thought that I knew what is missing…DRAMA! Drama was missing.

Everything seemed good. Maybe this is what a healthy relationship was supposed to feel like. Maybe NOTHING was missing at all, and this was totally normal. I had never had normal, so I decided to give it more time and listen for direction. Time went by, and I heard nothing, but I still couldn't shake this feeling that something just wasn't right.

One Sunday after church, I met him and told him that I wasn't ready to move forward in the relationship. He was crushed and kept asking why. I just didn't have the answer he was looking for.

Something just wasn't right. Now that I had been through counseling and had worked through some things, I realize that I had had that feeling in other relationships but had dismissed it. I felt bad for hurting him, but somehow, I knew ending it was the right thing to do.

I was in a good place. My life was good.

I was asked by my boss to be a panelist in one of our evening classes. People were going to ask specific questions regarding our experiences pertaining to overcoming adversity and gaining sustainable employment. It's funny that I don't remember much of the class or what was said, but what did stand out to me was that the panelist sitting right next me was the painter from my office.

He was quiet during most of the evening, and when it was his time to speak, I was really impressed with the wisdom that he had to offer. This guy had substance.

The next day at work, a call was transferred to my desk. I answered it, and it was a woman who I had coached several months back. She said she wanted to thank me for sharing my inspiring story on the panel. She went on to say that the man sitting next to me (the painter) had really been a blessing to her and what he had to say helped her so much. She went on and on about how she believed that God was speaking through him. We chatted a bit more and hung up. I sat there and thought what a blessing it was to work in such a great place.

Meanwhile, at home, I needed a change. I wanted to redecorate my house for a long time, and now I could afford to start the process. While talking to my office manager, I asked him if he knew anybody who would be interested in doing some work on my house. He mentioned the guy who had painted my office. He was friends with him and said he would find out if he was interested in the job. He was, and we set up an appointment for him to give me an estimate for the work I was looking for.

The day came for our appointment. I offered him a cup of coffee and a seat to talk about the work I needed, and the next thing I knew, it was three hours later.

His name was Dave. We had a great conversation, and when the subject of spiritual things came up, before we knew it, a couple of hours had passed by! I remember thinking he was a great guy and I could totally be friends with him. We had a good laugh about how long we had talked, and then he gave me an estimate on the work.

Over the next few weeks, we touched base a couple of times through text messaging. I caught myself laughing out loud on reading some of his texts, and I found myself coming right back with witty replies.

At one point, I thought he was flirting with me, but I wasn't sure. Was I getting a little intrigued? What was going on here—*was* this guy flirting with me? I decided to find out, so I came right out and asked him, and to my surprise he said, "Yes, I was!"

Now, I was intrigued. Something was going on—a spark had been lit between us, and it wasn't going out anytime soon.

He asked me if I would go out with him to lunch one day at work. We went and talked the entire time. It was obvious we were both excited to be around each other. We laughed and had a great time.

As he dropped me off after lunch, he mentioned seeing each other again. I decided to let him know where I stood in the dating department. I told him that I would really like that but also wanted to let him know that I would also be seeing other people. I told him I was taking the advice of the Christian psychologist whom I had been seeing.

Dave very calmly said, "I understand; go ahead and do what you feel you need to do, and I'll be right here waiting for you when you are finished with that. I'm not looking any further." I was taken aback by his response. He was OK with my decision to see other people, and he also let me know he wasn't going anywhere. I was impressed by his confidence and maturity.

When I came back from lunch, my office manager was standing in the hallway. He was staring at me with wide eyes, waiting to hear about my date with his friend. I told him we had a great time and would probably see each other again. He said he had a feeling this could really be something special.

I was starting to feel like that too but didn't want to be pushed around by my feelings or be impulsive. I had been there and done that, and had four other T-shirts.

I told him the details of our conversation and about what I said to Dave about seeing other people. He looked at me like I had two heads and asked why would I try to see other people. Why wouldn't I just see where this goes and forget everyone else, when this was going so great? I knew he meant well, but he didn't know everything that I had been through, and why this process needed to be different.

I wish I could tell you that I found lots of friends while fishing, but I didn't. Dave was the melon I was interested in; it became obvious to me that he was going to be my best friend.

After dating a while, to my surprise, everyone else was on board with my decision to pursue a relationship with him. I had support from everyone, even the people who I thought might be against it.

This man was kind, soft-spoken, and funny. We laughed so hard when we first met and still do to this very day. He is everything I have ever wanted and even some things I didn't know that I wanted. He is strong in the areas where I am weak and serves our family in the most selfless way. He is one of the wisest people I've ever met. He rarely gives his opinion, but when he does, you can bet nine out of ten times he will be right (ugh)!

I will always remember one special day after we were first married. He asked me to follow him in my car to drop off a work vehicle, and he would ride back with me. I agreed and he left in the work truck. A few minutes later as I was getting ready to leave to meet him, my phone rang. It was Dave.

He told me to stop at the gas station up the road because he just remembered my car needed fuel. He was turning around and driving back to meet me there so he could pump the gas for me. I said "OK," we hung up, and I stood there in silence.

This man was going to turn around, drive back to the gas station, and pump gas for me. Now, this may not seem like all that big of a deal to most people, but I was being shown that I was valued.

Dave just wanted to bless me and take care of me. I could count on one hand how many times I had to pump gas in the first couple of years. He wouldn't let me carry groceries or bags out of stores. He wanted to serve me.

I have never experienced love on an emotional level with anyone like I do with him. It became painfully obvious that I was going to let this man love me. I say painfully because I was going to let him all the way into my heart, and it was one of the most exciting but scariest things I have ever experienced. I read a quote somewhere that said, "Love is giving someone the power to destroy you but trusting them not to."

For me, opening my heart to this man was exhilarating and terrifying, and I was saying yes and diving all the way in.

There was a period for the first few months that we both felt physically sick being around each other. We experienced what it means to be lovesick. I never experienced anything so intense. God gave us both so much peace and confirmation about our relationship, and we knew we were supposed to be together.

Dave didn't have any children, and after a while, we decided to try. I had three miscarriages and an ectopic pregnancy while trying to conceive. It was a very difficult time in our lives. We shared the pain and adversity and got through it together. God used all of it to strengthen us. (Psalm 46:1 NIV)

We got pregnant shortly after the ectopic pregnancy and had a little boy to add to our tribe. He is the light of our world. It brought our family together and the older kids fell in love with our new family member.

His name is David. He is a delight, and we can't imagine our lives without him. It has been a gift from God to experience motherhood again. And this time to have a partner to share it with.

Dave and I have disagreements from time to time, like any other couple, and when we do, we work through them. Both of us work at resolving a conflict instead of fueling it. I am so grateful to God for His goodness and bringing Dave into my life.

CHAPTER 22
Who am I?

I WAS SITTING IN CHURCH ONE FRIDAY EVENING when a sweet, soft-spoken older woman walked up to me. Her smile and sparkling blue eyes were disarming. I saw her many times, but we never met. She gently reached out for my hands, and without a thought, I reached for hers.

We stood there holding hands for a moment, and what she said became another destiny marker in my life. She told me that as she was praying that morning, God put me on her heart. She said, "He told me to ask you this question: WHO ARE YOU?" She paused and smiled some more. I didn't have a response for that.

I was a bit concerned about God asking me a question. I heard it said before; God knows everything, and if He is asking you something, it's more than likely because you don't know the answer.

The answer to that question became my mission. How was I supposed to respond? What in the world was God up to, and how was I supposed to answer that question?

Who am I? What did He mean? I am a mom, a hairdresser, a Christian, um…OK, God, I give up! WHO AM I? Well, God didn't answer. I heard a whole lot of nothing. What I DID get was frustrated.

The first thing I did was call a couple of friends and tell them what happened. Each phone call ended with me asking them who they thought I was and how would they describe me. I asked them to just think about it, and if anything came to them they thought was significant, to please let me know. That question would not leave me for about two years. I never really felt like I could answer it.

At one point, I was looking at all the things I did, all the hats I wore, hoping that if I put them in the proper order of importance, it would give me the answer to who I was.

I couldn't get an answer from any of the people I turned to. So for the next couple of years, I kept that thought at the forefront of my mind. I looked for who I was in every area of my life. I never felt like I truly put my finger on it.

I kept asking the Lord to show me WHAT I was going to do for Him specifically. If I could just find the answer to that, then I would know who I was. The answer was nowhere in sight.

I had all but laid the question down and stopped searching until one morning, I opened my eyes as the sun started coming up in my bedroom and these words came into my mind: "IT'S NOT ABOUT WHAT YOU DO; IT'S WHO YOU ARE." And with those simple words came an understanding, and the pieces started coming together for me. I got it.

It doesn't matter what I do, when I know who I am. I can be who He made me to be in every situation and every setting. It doesn't matter what I'm doing. It matters who I am. The doing will just come. Doing will come out of being.

Whatever I find myself doing doesn't matter as much as my relationship with the Father. First and foremost, I am His child. That revelation settled something in me once and for all. I was accepted in Him. (Ephesians 1:6 NKJV) I was good because He says so.

For too long, I had been looking in the wrong direction for approval or acceptance from people, and when I was rejected, I assumed I wasn't good. Performance-based love says I must *do* to be good or right. I should act a certain way, or do the right things to be approved.

I needed better love than that. The never-ending kind. Love says I want you just like you are, right now, and forever.

I finally stopped asking the Lord what I was going to be doing for Him and started being who I was in Him—and it changed everything. •

I was settled; the identity crisis was over. I had been rejected by men, friends, family, and church people over the years. It was always painful, but as I look back, some of my pain was caused by my behavior. None of it was pleasant, but it was all necessary, and even good for me.

As good as my marriage is with Dave, we went through a period for a couple of years where I felt rejected by him. It was a hard time for me, but it would also be the final blow to the spirit of rejection in my life.

We both loved Jesus and were sold out to living our lives as believers, but we often viewed Christianity through different filters. We were on different sides of the swimming pool, so to speak.

Sometimes, when I shared with him what I felt God was speaking or showing me, I would notice that it was out of his comfort zone—he would get quiet and even smug.

Those same old rejection feelings would arise in me and try to come back again. It happened enough that I eventually stopped sharing with him and started to withdraw from anything spiritual around him. As time went on, everything seemed to be good in all areas of our lives, except that one area. He seemed to accept everything about me, unless it pertained to spiritual gifts or supernatural encounters.

It was during this time that I shut down and stopped being me. I had been rejected by church people for who I was, and I couldn't go through it again, not with Dave.

I shut down and hid. I started resenting Dave underneath the surface. I suffered for months until I finally came to the realization that trying to hide who I was to please someone else was codependency. •

God made me, and I am good. It didn't matter who rejects me; God doesn't. Not only that, He delights in me. (Psalm 149:4 NIV) Even if He was the only one, I had to hold on to that. I knew I was God's child. So why was I feeling this way?

In the past, I shared spiritual things with people I shouldn't have shared. Some would slowly pull away from me, some totally rejected me, some were jealous. I operated in prophesy, words of knowledge, healing, and deliverance, but I needed wisdom and maturity. I needed to learn that I couldn't share everything with everyone.

The book of Genesis tells the story of a young man named Joseph who suffered extreme rejection.

Joseph's father loved him deeply and at times seemed to favor him among his other siblings. He was a dreamer. He dreamed of greatness. His father gave him a robe as a special gift one day; this caused jealousy to arise in some of the brothers. They couldn't stand Joseph. The more he tried to relate to them, the worse things seemed to get for him. They saw the favor that their father bestowed upon Joseph and hated him for it.

One day, he shared a dream with some of the brothers. He shared how the dream ended with all the family eventually bowing down to him. With jealousy already at work, the brothers hated him even more.

He had a second dream, and instead of keeping it to himself, he not only shared with the brothers, but told his father too. This time, Joseph's father intervened and rebuked him. He questioned the nature of his dream by asking him if he thought that the entire family was actually going to bow down to the ground before him.

The brothers plotted against Joseph and mapped out a plan to eliminate him. They set a trap for him to fall into. They planned to kill him and make up a story that he was eaten by a wild animal.

When Joseph showed up at the scene, the first thing they did was strip him of his precious robe and then they threw him into a pit. After a long hard day of kidnapping their little brother, they sat down for a bite to eat.

As they were eating, they saw a caravan headed toward Egypt. One of the brothers had a moment of clarity and talked the other brothers into sparing Joseph's life. He explained there was no gain in killing him when they could sell him and profit.

So they sold him into slavery for twenty shekels of silver to the caravan headed for Egypt. They took his special robe, dipped it in blood to make it look like he had been killed, and went home to give their father the news. (Genesis 37:3-32 NIV)

That's some serious rejection, wouldn't you say? Thank the Lord that the story doesn't end there. Our God always settles the score. If God put a dream inside you, nobody can stop it.

And nobody could stop Joseph's dream either. God put those dreams inside him, and they were coming to pass whether his brothers liked it or not. God was with Joseph, and if God be for you, who can be against you? (Rom 8:31 KJV)

Joseph had to face much more adversity on the way to the fulfillment of his dreams. There was a purpose that he was born for, and God was going to use all the adversity to bring forth that purpose.

Every place of adversity was a place of training. Joseph ended up excelling and finding favor as a slave; he was put in charge of his master's house until the master's wife accused him of a crime he didn't commit, and he was thrown into prison.

While in prison, he interpreted dreams for the Pharaoh's former employees who were incarcerated as well. One of them was exonerated, and his position was restored as Pharaoh's butler once again. (Genesis 39:2-21; 40:1-18 NIV)

Joseph excelled and found favor in every situation. His gifts made room for him. (Proverbs 18:16).

Time passed, and Pharaoh had a couple of dreams that troubled him. The former inmate, whose position as butler was restored, told the him that he knew someone who could interpret dreams.

Joseph was brought before Pharaoh and interpreted his dreams. They were very serious dreams telling of a great famine that would come to the land. As a result of Joseph's interpretation, Pharaoh removed Joseph from prison and appointed him second in command in all of Egypt.

With this new knowledge, they prepared for a great famine. Everything Joseph predicted came to pass. Eventually, the famine caused Joseph's family to search for food for their very survival, and they headed to Egypt. The same brothers who tried to destroy him now needed him. Joseph eventually revealed himself to his brothers, and restoration began. The fulfillment of Joseph's dream came to pass. (Genesis 41; 42:1-3 NIV)

Over the years, I've had great men and women of God speak into my life. I have had the same prophetic words given to me by people that have never met, but the words they spoke over me were the same. I've had visions and dreams pertaining to my destiny that quite honestly blew my mind. In saying that, it has been a battle to hold on to those words, when I would see the exact opposite happening.

One afternoon, I was sitting alone in my living room, pondering these things and decided to have a serious conversation with the Lord about it. It went something like this:

Lord, I've been standing and holding onto these words and the things I thought You showed me. It's been years. Maybe some of things I've been believing are made up. Maybe I think higher of myself than I ought to with these things that I "see" for my future. Maybe it's all in vain.

If that is the case, I am so sorry. Please forgive me and help me to get back on track. Today, I lay all those things down, and I'm handing them over to You.

I was sincere, and it hurt. I had been standing for a long time, and maybe it was all in vain. I decided at that moment to lay all of those things down and move forward from there and see where God leads me.

I had all but forgotten about that simple prayer when a few days later, Dave walked in with a serious look on his face. He said, "I need to talk to you." I stopped what I was doing, and he came over and sat down by me.

He said, "I think I have a word for you from God." Now he had my full attention. Those are words that I have never heard come out of his mouth. His face told me he was wasn't joking. "OK," I said, "What is it?"

He went on to say that he felt uncomfortable telling me this, and I could tell he was. I was always the one coming in talking about hearing something from God. He said, "I was reading in my Bible about Joseph. When my eyes looked at the words 'Joseph dreamed of greatness,' I felt like God spoke to me...about you." I just stared at him. He went on to say, "I felt like God told me that you are like Joseph. There is greatness inside you, and those things that you have seen for your life are from Him. He put them there."

The next few words had me undone. He said, "None of it is in *vain*. And the people who rejected you in the church were like Joseph's brothers. And I have been like one of Joseph's brothers to you too, and need to ask you to forgive me."

No one knew what I had prayed that day in my living room. God was with me, listening to every word.

I just cupped my hands over my face and wept. No words can describe this God we serve. And I was now wrecked for Him all over again.

God, in His perfect time, will bring healing and restoration to every area of our lives. He will perfect those things that concern us. (Psalm 138:8)

Epilogue

MY MOM USED TO TELL A STORY EVERY NOW AND then. She usually told it when she was sitting around talking with other women about how they found out they were pregnant. I was very small the first time I heard it.

She hadn't been feeling well and went to the doctor. After the examination, he said, "YEP, there's definitely a varmint in there; you are pregnant."

My mom said she immediately started sobbing. She would then make the sobbing noises for special effect, and everyone hearing it would laugh.

She only meant it to be a funny story of her response to the news of having to go through the oncoming woes of pregnancy while already having an active toddler, but that's not what I heard.

When I heard the story, I had a much different reaction. I felt shame.

I thought that because she sobbed, it meant that she didn't really want to be pregnant with me.

She would have never told the story back then if she would have known the impact it had on me as a little girl. Today I know she loves me very much. I also know that the enemy uses any chance he can get to gain access into our lives, even from the womb.

He doesn't care how, when, or where, as long as he gets in. His nature is to kill, steal, and destroy. If something is being stolen from you, trying to destroy you, or trying to kill you, you can bet that it is rooted in darkness. (John 10:10 NIV) He is merciless, if he finds a wound, a way, or has a "right" to come in, he is going to take the opportunity.

Rejection hindered me my entire life until I went through deliverance. I fought a good fight and stood my ground, resisting the lies of rejection. I spent years renewing my mind to the truth of God's word, but it always seemed like something was still there.

Until deliverance, it was like I had been playing whack-a-mole with a spirit of rejection. It would pop up somewhere in my life, and I would try to hit it on the head to get rid of it.

It wouldn't be long before it would show up somewhere else, and I'd whack it again, but I could never truly get free.

All of that would change when Dave and I signed up for deliverance ministry.

It was a weekend retreat, with training and equipping before the deliverance session. The ministry ran like a well-oiled machine.

During our session, there were eight prayer warriors seated around us with notepads and pens. They were instructed to seek the Lord about what the chief and ruling demonic spirit was over our lives. After about 10 minutes, the leader asked if everyone had written something down and were ready to discuss it.

After Dave was ministered to, it was my turn. They went around the circle sharing pictures and words that they felt like God gave them. Six out of eight people heard the exact same thing for me! Those six said the same words, "spirit of rejection." (2 Corinthians 13:1 NKJV)

When it was time for the last girl to share, she also had a picture to describe.

She said, "I also heard 'spirit of rejection' when I was praying, and I saw a picture of a little girl in a sundress, whirling around in a beautiful field with not a care in the world. Out of nowhere, a big bad wolf grabbed her by the ankles and pulled her into the woods."

What she said hit my wound right dead in the center. It was a perfect picture of what the molestation did to me. I felt pain and tried to control myself from crying too loud, but I was openly weeping.

The man leading the group then prayed over me peacefully, broke the assignment off my life, and commanded that spirit and any spirits under that one to leave and never return in the name of Jesus.

The next day, during an educational session, the founder of the ministry spoke. Everyone who had went through deliverance was there. He talked to us about all the different spirits we had been set free from.

When he started talking about the spirit of rejection, he made a comment I will never forget. He said, "Those who get free from the spirit of rejection usually come out golden in the area of dominion."

I almost fell out of my chair. There it was again. Dominion.

That sentence brought me back to the day I was in my car when God said He was going to teach me Dominion. I was speechless.

All through my life, I had been rejected by people. It seemed every relationship was affected by it and would eventually come to an end. It was an assignment on my life that stole so much from me.

Now, I have friends coming out of the woodwork, and there is such a change in the way people respond to me. People pay attention to the things I say. The difference is night and day.

Once, as I was sharing something at a Bible study, everyone started grabbing their notebooks and pens to write down what I was saying. When I realized what they were doing, I almost laughed out loud. (Proverbs 3:4 NIV)

The assignment of rejection was broken off my life.

Please hear me: it doesn't matter what is coming against you; you can be free. If you've been walking with the Lord and struggling, or even battling something for years, freedom is your right. The Lord came to set us free and give us life. He's a supernatural God with all power and authority, and He has made it possible for you to be whole. He's been delivering people from the hands of their enemies since people started walking around on this earth. It's who He is— Our God is a deliverer!

We are made up of three parts: body, soul, and spirit. (1 Thessalonians 5:23 NIV)

Our soul is the realm of our being where we feel everything, and it's also an area where the enemy loves to fight us. It is made up of our mind, will, and emotions. It's the area where we can feel anger, lust, depression, anxiety, love, and all the other feelings. The area where we can process information, make a decision, and act on it. It's the area where we have a free will to choose. Like when we choose to accept Jesus. No wonder the enemy fights us so hard here!!!

If our soul has been wounded, he will take up residence in that wound and cause trouble until he is removed. In the same way that an open wound is susceptible to bacterial infection, wounds in our soul are susceptible to demonic infestation. They need to be tended to, cleaned out, and the appropriate medicine applied.

God has given us authority over ALL the works of darkness. (Luke 10:19 NIV)

Sin and death have been defeated forever. Jesus took the keys of death and hell. (Revelation 1:18 NIV) He has given those keys to us, along with the authority to use them.

"And I tell you that you are Peter, and on this rock, I will build my church, and the gates of Hades will not overcome it. I will give you the keys of the Kingdom of heaven; whatsoever you bind on earth will be bound in heaven, and whatever you loose on earth will be loosed in heaven." (Matthew 16:18-19 NIV)

In the beginning, He made man in His image and likeness, and said, "Let them have Dominion." (Genesis 1:26 ESV) It was bestowed upon man the day He created them. It came with our package, so to speak. It means to rule and reign.

Man walked in freedom and had perfect communion with God, until sin and death entered the world, and man lost Dominion. We were now subject to sin, sickness, and death. (Genesis 3:6-24 NIV)

You and I were born into that fallen state. God sent His Son to redeem and deliver us from the kingdom of darkness.

Jesus stretched out his arms on the cross and said, "IT IS FINISHED." (John 19:30 NKJV) The work was finished. We now have the authority to take back Dominion.

We are to be about our Father's business praying for His Kingdom to come, His will to be done, on earth as it is in heaven. (Matthew 6:10 NIV)

It starts with the church. He sets us free, so we can apply that finished work and give it to others.

His Bride is getting cleaned up and prepared to meet her Bridegroom to rule and reign with Him.

"That He might present to Himself a glorious church, not having spot, or wrinkle, or any such thing; but that it should be holy and without blemish." (Ephesians 5:27 KJV)

It is time for us to take back everything that has been stolen from us, and walk in this thing called Dominion in every area of our lives.

"Arise, shine; for your light has come, and the glory of the Lord has risen upon you. For behold, darkness will cover the earth, and deep darkness the peoples; but the Lord will rise upon you and His glory will appear upon you." (Isaiah 60:1-2 NASB)